Transformations

*Teen Mothers Journey
to Success*

authored and edited by
Karen M. McCord & Ella Clark-Tolliver

Azimuth
The Azimuth Press

Azimuth
4041 Bowman
Box 211
Macon, GA 31210

ISBN 1-886218-12-9

Copyright © 2000 by Karen McCord & Ella Tolliver. All rights reserved. No part of this book may be used or reproduced in any manner whatsoever without the written permission of the editors. For further information, contact **Transformations**, P. O. Box 702, Suisun, CA 94585; Phone: (707) 428-4423 or e-mail: *teenmominfo@aol.com*

Second Printing

Excerpts from the women of 'Transformations'

"Quintin motivated me to go on. I really felt that I needed to do for him because he was my choice. I want to work for special needs children's issues to give families what they really need and to educate schools on the needs of children. We have not done enough to help."
from The Antoinette Williams Story

"My greatest blessings in life, my greatest gifts in life, my greatest joys in life have been my children. My children motivate me to keep going. I wanted a better life for them. My advice to teen moms is to never give up. Don't let anyone determine who you are. Life is really what you make it."

"I climbed Mt. Fuji in Japan with my 14-year-old daughter. It is 12,000 feet high. My daughter complained the whole time. It took us approximately six hours to reach the top. When we finally arrived at the top, my daughter said, "Wow! Mom, I'm really glad that we did it." Life will present you with mountains to climb. Just keep putting one foot in front of the other and keep going."
from The Inez Guillory Story

"There were obstacles then, but now, I look back on them as challenges. I kept telling myself: NO ONE IS GOING TO TELL ME WHAT I CANNOT DO. I wasn't going to let anything or anyone stop me. People expected me to fail — expected me not to make it."

"My advice to teen moms is to climb over every obstacle that comes your way. Don't move it. Once you climb over it, the next one that comes will be easier to climb."
from The Delphine Metcalf Story

"My key to success has been my determination — not letting anyone tell me that I couldn't. I wanted to get out of my mother's house. It was my biggest motivation. I was motivated by the reality of having to provide for my kids and having to pay my bills."
from The Angela Young Story

"It is possible for them to achieve the things that they want out of life as long as they work hard. Their primary responsibility is to take care of their children. By taking care of their children, by doing the things that they need to do academically, and by working wisely, all things are possible."

from The Ramona Garrett Story

"A challenge for me was not giving up on myself; I never had the opportunity to grow as a woman. I was growing up and raising a kid at the same time. You can't change yesterday, but you can definitely change tomorrow."

from The Karen Garcia Story

"The biggest impact of having a child so young was that I never got to have fun. I never got to party or go out with friends. I wanted my child to have the things in life that I never had. I had to get out and work to accomplish that. Currently, my children are fifteen and nineteen. We are now in our nineteenth year of marriage. Life is good."

from The Linda MacFall Story

"My greatest challenge was being a mother, a wife, and a student. My parents did not turn away from me. They continued to parent. I am sure that it was very difficult for them, but they continued to love. That really made the difference for us."

from The Vivian Hazzard Story

DEDICATION

Karen's Dedication

This book is lovingly dedicated to the memory of my late parents, **Milus Moddis McCord** and **Margaret Wallace McCord** - and to my late granddaughter, **Saniyah Danielle McCord.**

Also to my grandchildren: **Joseph, Jamel, Sekye, Elijah,** and **Caleb.**

Ella's Dedication

This book is lovingly dedicated to the memory of my late parents, **Harry** and **Josephine Clark,** for constantly providing growth opportunities and for their unconditional love and nurturing.

Also to my grandchildren: **Greg, Jr.**, **Christopher, Charnae, Marcus, Bree, Tarajah, Jude,** and **Indurian.**

ACKNOWLEDGMENTS

Bringing this project to completion has been a challenging task; "To God be the Glory." In addition to the Almighty, we thank the following individuals and organization:

- *Mary Park, collaborator and interviewer, for her diligent work and commitment to assisting us with this project;*

- *Michael Lawson for his willingness to share his legal expertise;*

- *Marnie McLeod and Olivia Jomoc for their technical assistance.*

- *Denise Mitchell Smith, our editor, for bringing the language of our stories together for the printed page.*

- *Nina and Mychal Wynn for their encouragement.*

- *Carol Lilliberg for believing in the project.*

- *Milt Combs who believed in both of us as students and who continues to support and encourage our professional growth and development*

-*Bill Thurston who taught us to continue to strive for excellence.*

- *and Solano Community College for supporting the research presented in this material.*

Karen's Special Thanks

To my children: Songhai Deveaux, Sylvia and Sylvester McCord, and my son-in-law Glenn Deveaux for making me proud, for the love and support they have shown me through the years, and for bringing me immeasurable joy.

To my siblings: Joseph, Charles, Curtis, and Juanita McCord for the love and understanding they have shown me through the years.

To my elders, Vilma France and Betty Buckner for sharing wisdom.

To my ex-husband, Darryl Clare, for supporting the telling of our story.

To my dear friends Sandra Mattavous Frye, Inez Falconer, and Sherri Burwell for helping me sort out life and come to terms with my life experiences.

To Duane Smith, whose steadfast love and support have greatly contributed to the completion of this project.

To my dear friend Janice Brice, whose life experiences provided the motivation and inspiration for this book.

Ella's Special Thanks

To my God-ordained mate, John, for over 37 years of true love and devotion.

To my three adult children: Vivian Hazzard, John Jr., and Lisa Williams.

To my wonderful sons-in-law: Gregory Hazzard, Sr. and Charles Williams.

To my brothers Preston and Kenneth and their wives Virginia and Christine.

To my sister and role model, Harriett.

CONTENTS

About the Authors/Editors

Foreword

A Date with Destiny   1
    The Karen McCord Story - *Professor/Consultant*

I Never Thought This Could Happen   18
    The Antoinette Williams Story - *Social Worker*

Date Rape   24
    The Inez Guillory Story - *Captain, United States Air Force*
    The Delphine Metcalf Story – *Retired United States Army/Student*

The High School Young Mothers Program   42
    The Dana Littlepage Story - *Registered Nurse*
    The Michelle Wallace Story - *Bank/Human Resources Specialist*

Babies Having Babies   60

    The LaRahna Martin Story - *Accountant/Business Owner*
    The Angela Young Story - *X-Ray Technician*

College Campus Baby   67
    The Nicole Howell Story – *Medical School Student*
    The Ramona Garrett Story – *Chief Judge Superior Court*

Songs in the Key of Life   82
    The Karen Garcia Story – *Case Manager*
    The Linda MacFall Story – *Crisis Intervention Manager*

Mother and Daughter, Happily Ever After   93
    The Vivian Hazzard Story – *Registered Nurse*
    The Ella Tolliver Story – *College Dean/Counselor*

Epilogue   111
    "Living Life"
    "A Look in the Mirror"

ABOUT THE AUTHORS/EDITORS

Born in New York City and raised in housing projects located in the South Bronx, *Karen M. McCord*, the fourth of five children was labeled "gifted" in elementary school. She excelled academically until a series of life experiences led her to give up on formal education, dropping out of high school at age 16. She briefly attended continuation school, subsequently passing the General High School Equivalency examination. She attended Long Island University on a full-tuition scholarship until she became pregnant at the age of 18. She moved to California in 1974.

In California, she resumed her educational development, earning an A.A. degree in African-American Studies from Solano Community College. From there she went on to earn her B.S. degree in Human Relations and Organizational Behavior and a Master's degree in Counseling, both from the University of San Francisco. Karen specializes in Cultural Competency Training, Gender Bias Issues, and Multicultural Education as an independent consultant. She has a distinguished career in human services and is an Ethnic Studies/Psychology Professor at Solano Community College. She is a frequent speaker on Women's Empowerment Issues, Cultural Competency and Sexual Harassment for organizations throughout the country. Karen is at work on a collection of personal essays tentatively entitled *Reflections*.

Ella Tolliver, Ph.D., is a native Californian, the youngest of four children. Her work experience includes teaching in public and private schools, college staff development and counseling, with more than 20 years of experience as a specialist in interpersonal effectiveness training. She is currently Dean of Counseling and Disabled Students Programs and Services (DSPS) at Solano Community College in Northern California.

Ella has earned a Ph.D. in Education and a Master's degree in Counseling and Mental Health. She has held a variety of leadership positions and is a sought after speaker by a variety of organizations and churches. Her article, "Think High and Walk Tall," was published in the <u>1998 Women's Spiritual Devotional Book.</u> Ella is currently working on a collection of memoirs.

FOREWORD

There is a definite stigma associated with teen pregnancy. Many former teen mothers who have become successful later on in their lives are reluctant to share their stories. This, no doubt, contributes to the lack of positive role models linked to this subject. In the 1980's, statistics indicated that 13% of teenaged moms completed high school. Many had no plans for pursing college. Today, only one third of teenaged mothers complete high school per the "National Campaign to Prevent Teen Pregnancy." Rather than continuing to study the 87% to 66%, who do not complete their education, this book focuses on those who *do* complete their education and it identifies the factors that have enabled their success. There also appears to be value in having successful individuals, who were once teen moms, share their stories so that those in similar circumstances might be encouraged and empowered to change their lives.

This collection of stories by no means promotes teenaged pregnancy. Most teen mothers agree that it is far better to wait for parenthood. However, once pregnancy has occurred and a child has been born, the options for training and education must be afforded to young mothers to ensure their success. Programs need to be developed. Educators and society at-large need to know what to do in order to tailor programs and services to meet their needs. Much of what has been written with respect to teenaged pregnancy focuses on the larger percentage of teen moms who do not make it through high school and who have difficulty making critical life adjustments. Focusing on negatives helps to define the problem, but it does not help to identify proven solutions.

Teenagers are having babies and we, as a society, are paying for it in numerous ways, including government taxes and other poverty assistance programs. Statistics have shown that male children born to teenaged moms are 13% more likely to end up in prison.

This book is about teenaged mothers who have become successful, functioning, self-supporting adults. The idea for this project came to me around 1988. At that time, my own daughter had become pregnant at the age of 16 and I was concerned about the lack of positive inspirational information available to teen parents. My daughter returned from a doctor's appointment one day and described a poster on teenage pregnancy that said, "She'll never go to the prom. She'll never finish school." She expressed her frustration by the message on the poster and asked, "Why not? Why can't a teen mom finish school?" We both had the immediate reference of individuals whom we had known, personally, who had become teenaged mothers and who had continued to pursue their goals, resulting in the achievement of success in their chosen fields.

I felt that it was unfortunate that others in similar circumstances had not had readily-available positive role models. Many young mothers, like the one depicted on the poster, thought that their lives were over and tended to give up, limiting themselves and their children to lives of poverty and dependency. My daughter, from the beginning, knew that she would continue to pursue her goals. However, she acknowledged that it might need to be done differently.

The Young Mothers Program at the school where my daughter attended indicated that they did not have a single former student who had gone on to a four-year college. We made it clear that although my daughter was pregnant, she would still be going to college. My daughter's Godmother had been a teen mom herself and had graduated from law school, becoming a partner in a firm by age 30. At 38, she was a Judge. My daughter reaped the benefit of knowing that she could still pursue her dreams. Great for my daughter! But I couldn't help but be concerned about the young people for whom there were no immediately identifiable positive and inspiring role models. I decided, at that time, to seek out other teen mothers who had achieved professional and personal success and who were willing to share their stories.

I shared this goal with my colleague, Ella Tolliver, and we began to collaborate on this collection of stories. *Transformations* is a compilation of personal stories of women who were once teen mothers; women who have gone on to achieve exceptional educational, professional, and career goals.

Karen M. McCord

A Date with Destiny

The Karen McCord Story

Karen McCord is one of the co-editors of this book. She is a college professor and consultant. Karen is an African-American mother of three adult children, grandmother of six, and lives in Northern California.

At nineteen, I received one of my greatest gifts in life — my daughter, Songhai. She has been a miracle, a blessing, and a joy to know. She remains one of the most consistent people in my life. She has taught me the true meaning of unconditional love and she has loved me unconditionally, bringing new dimensions to my life from the day she took her first breath. She has provided countless new reasons for living, hope for the future, inspiration when I have needed it most, and understanding when others had no clue! My mother always said, "Songhai was the best thing that ever happened to you." Initially, I didn't know what she meant by that statement.

I don't ever remember wanting children. I didn't even play much with dolls, growing up. However, I clearly remember wanting this pregnancy. It was a very smooth pregnancy and delivery. I remember my water breaking at home as we were preparing to go to a movie. The ride from the Bronx to Harlem Hospital in Manhattan was rather uneventful with one sharp pain while we crossed the bridge. When we arrived at the hospital, I refused a wheel chair, but they insisted that I ride in the wheelchair anyway. The doctor examined me quickly, then stated to the nurse, "Admit her." I immediately asked, "For what?" "You're about to have the baby," he replied.

I couldn't believe it. I was not in significant pain and the baby wasn't due for three weeks. I had gone to my scheduled prenatal appointment that very morning. Friends who had given birth previously told me that when the labor hit, I would know from the pain. I felt some discomfort, but I never felt the excruciating pain they had described. Within two hours of leaving home, Songhai Tanayi entered the world. Because Darryl and I were not married, he was not allowed in the labor or delivery room. I would have wanted him to be with me. Instead, my daughter was delivered in a room full of strangers.

My first twenty-one years were spent in New York City. New York is a fascinating city and I have come to appreciate the many benefits of life there. New York was a challenging place for me to come of age. My parents were always employed. My mother, who was from West Virginia, was college educated and employed as a dietitian at a local hospital. My father was employed by the United States Postal Service. He was raised in Birmingham, Alabama. During most of the time I lived in New York, I lived in the South Bronx in Saint Mary's Projects.

The projects were located in the middle of what became known as "Fort Apache," a war zone, and an urban battleground. My soldiers were my three older brothers and friends. In addition to my brothers, I also had one younger sister. There is almost a decade between my younger sister and me. As a result, I don't recall her being a significant part of my growing-up years.

St. Mary's Projects was somewhat of an oasis. Where I lived, 99 percent of the adult residents were employed and not on welfare. There were roaches, but no rats. Surrounding our twenty-one story building was green grass, trees, well-kept shrubs, and a park for children to play in. It wasn't until much later in my life I learned that I had lived in the "ghetto." I never felt poor and our parents were able to provide the necessities of life and more.

When I discovered I was pregnant, I was nearing the end of my third semester at Long Island University (LIU). I was attending LIU on a full scholarship, which included books and tuition. The fact that I was even in college at the time was somewhat amazing. I dropped out of high school when I was sixteen and never went any further than the ninth grade. I took and passed the GED about five months after I dropped out. Less than a year later (at seventeen) I started college on a full scholarship. I also began living in the dorm during my freshman year.

I was very independent and did not rely on my parents for much. I don't remember my parents' reaction to the news that I was pregnant. I was already independent. When I announced my pregnancy, I also informed them of my plans to establish a household with my baby's father. My pregnancy did not impact my family a lot, because I was already pretty much on my own.

My child's father, whom I later married, was also a student at the college. We met through his friend, whom I had previously dated. We were seeing each other intensely for about eight months when I became pregnant. I clearly remember Darryl's reaction to the news that I was pregnant. He initially wanted me to consider abortion, however I would not. Abortion was out of the question. I'd had an abortion earlier that year. That was a difficult and somewhat forced decision. I was never comfortable with that choice and knew from the beginning that I would have this child. I wanted this child! I was also convinced that I was going to have this child with or without his support, although I must admit that I desperately wanted his support and felt relieved when he offered it.

It took Darryl a few days to absorb the news. He disappeared from my life for about a week. When I didn't hear from him, I decided to find him. I located him as he left his job one afternoon and he told me that he would stick with me through this pregnancy. We began making plans for our future together.

    We located an apartment through my friend Janice, who knew someone who managed apartment buildings. Friends and family also helped us to furnish our first apartment. Janice called one day and told us that a sofa had been discarded in their trash dumpster. We quickly went to claim it. Darryl and I brought our "new" sofa home and used Lysol and fabric shampoo to make it usable. We did not have a phone or a TV. We lived in a studio apartment and Darryl supported us financially.

    Initially, I planned to continue going to school throughout the pregnancy, however that quickly changed. I remember going to class one day and deciding that I had no desire to continue with my classes. I didn't put a lot of thought into leaving school. One day in biology class, the formaldehyde just made me sick. We were dissecting fetal pigs and it was too much for me. There were only three weeks left in the semester, but I had decided that I needed to leave — not just biology, but *everything*. I went from professor to professor requesting to drop my classes.

    Not one professor asked me why I was leaving school. They simply signed my drop card. Not one professor suggested an alternative. No one really seemed to care. It was as if I had fulfilled their expectations that I would not succeed — that I would become just another statistic. I did inquire about my scholarship and I was told that my scholarship would be held for up to one year, so I knew that I would have the option of returning to school. I didn't know it would be so hard! I never returned to LIU.

Looking back, the thing that I feel I missed out on the most as a result of my pregnancy was playing college basketball. I loved playing basketball. After riding the bench the previous semester, it looked like I might have earned a starting position. I had spent the summer at a camp as a Girls' Athletic Director and had played basketball all summer. I returned to school a much-improved player. The coach and my teammates seemed very impressed and I was thrilled with my new skill level.

Basketball was the only dream that really died as a result of my pregnancy. Darryl and I played pickup basketball games at the beach and around the city until I was about six months pregnant. He'd get the ball, throw it to me, and I would shoot! People we met were amazed, first of all, because I was female and secondly, because I was pregnant. I didn't want to give up basketball, but eventually, I did.

My prenatal care was provided through Harlem Hospital in New York City. It was during one of my first appointments that the nurse, upon finding out that I was a college student, asked me the complexion of the baby's father. I thought that this was an odd question, but I responded anyway. When I told her that he was light-skinned, she said to me that it would be easy to find a home for a "light" baby and advised me not to throw away my life by having a child at this time. She stated that she felt that I had potential and that a baby would ruin my hopes of having a good life. She suggested that both Darryl and I should continue our education and make something of our lives.

I left the hospital feeling very alone, hurt, angry, and overwhelmed by life. I was still determined to have and keep this child. I knew then that I would eventually complete college. Many years later, I found out that I was unable to conceive any more children. Songhai would be my only birth child. I'm glad that I followed my inner feelings and instincts. To this day, I believe that this child was meant to live. Darryl and I both continued our education. He earned a doctorate degree and I have a Master's degree. It was challenging, but education continued to be important for both of us and we accomplished our educational goals.

I first came to California in the early 1970's with six boxes, one child, little money, and the dream of creating a different life for my child. Why California? Well, before permanently relocating to California, my daughter had been kidnapped from New York. I had located her 3,000 miles away in Berkeley, California. She was with her father who was living with another woman and her child. The children were being passed off as twins.

To make a long story short, I had gone to California to retrieve her. While there, Darryl and I talked and decided to put the past behind us. We agreed that California offered greater opportunities for our family. I returned to New York just long enough to give notice on my job, bid my farewells, and pack. I left all that was familiar to me and came to California following a dream. California was the land we used to sing about when I attended Camp Minisink as a teenager:

> *There lies a world beyond these mountains,*
> *There lies a world for us to see,*
> *And we must go beyond these mountains;*
> *Dear Lord, help us to walk with thee!*

Yes, this was the world I needed to explore. California took me beyond the mountains. I knew in my spirit that California would be the place where my dreams and the dreams I had yet to dream would come true! The circumstances were not ideal. However, California appeared to offer more than New York. I can remember standing outside of the apartment building in Berkeley where Darryl and this woman were living and wondering what I would be taking Songhai back to in New York.

It was a perfect California day. The sun was shining brightly and hope filled the air. The three-story building where they lived seemed to offer so much more than the projects where I had lived in New York. Darryl was Songhai's father and although he had betrayed me, I felt the need to give the relationship another chance on different soil. I knew that he loved our child. I wanted to believe that he loved me, too. I saw a new world in California. I saw opportunities and I wanted to see more. I felt that we could overcome any obstacles, and for the most part, we did!

I knew that I did not want Songhai to be an only child. I also knew that at nineteen I was not in a position to have any more children right away. So I conceded early on that I would most likely adopt when the time came to have more children. In December 1979, we welcomed Sylvia and Sylvester into our family. Sylvester was eight months younger than Songhai and Sylvia was exactly one year older than Songhai; they share the same birthday.

Darryl and I stayed together for about nine years, totally. We were great friends, had much in common and enjoyed exploring life, sharing and growing together. He was the first person with whom I shared my childhood pain of being raped. We became very close but it just wasn't enough. We were young and inexperienced and there were so many women in his life. I could tell that he felt very restricted by marriage and needed room to grow. At some point, we became weighted by the demands of life and we decided to separate and divorce. Although the marriage did not survive, the friendship did and our daughter has the benefit of having two parents who love and respect each other although they divorced.

I have basically raised my children as a single parent without any consistent financial support from Darryl. I do not resent his lack of financial support because, I believe as a result of the circumstances, I became a stronger individual. I certainly feel that all absent parents have a financial responsibility to support their children. However, I recall the disappointment of waiting for his check and not being able to feed my children. I realized then, during the first few months of our separation, that I would not spend my life waiting for his check. I became even more determined, and never needed his check for food again. On the occasions when he sent money, we didn't need it for necessities.

My support system consisted of my entire family. Darryl's brother, Eric, has always been supportive. Throughout the years, my support system has assisted me financially and emotionally. When I was single and struggling with three young children, my father would always purchase their school supplies and he would take us out to dinner every Monday. My mother helped in any way that she could. Eric, Rheuhama and my sister, Juanita, frequently provided respite care. My brothers, Joe, Charles, and Curtis never turned down my requests for money.

Friends always provided an ear when I was struggling with the challenges of raising three children alone. I really felt that I had already survived the worst: a rape at thirteen, the kidnapping of my daughter, divorcing the man I still loved. What could be worse? Life could only get better.

My major challenges were finances and education. I divorced and returned to school full time during the same year. Returning to school was not a difficult decision. I simply looked at my options and the decision was easy. To support the lifestyle that I had become accustomed to, I needed a job that paid much better than minimum wage. I realized quickly that a college degree would provide more opportunities for me. I did not want to move out of my house and I did not want to live in substandard housing again.

I had visions of the roaches and mice that shared the apartment with Darryl and I in the Bronx. I was determined not to live with roaches or jump over mice ever again. A college degree was critical to support what I wanted for my children and myself. I was also determined not to depend upon anyone to support my lifestyle or to feed my children. Yes, I needed an education and a good-paying job.

During fleeting moments, I began to think that it was too difficult to parent three children and go to school full-time while working full-time. But, I only needed to flash back to the mice I had to dodge on the way to the bathroom at night when I was pregnant with Songhai. It was awful! I was scared. Sometimes there would be dead mice on the floor that the dog had killed.

Alternatively, my thoughts would traverse to the roaches that shared another apartment with us. When Songhai was a baby, I would get up to get her a bottle at night. I would turn on the light and wait patiently by the entryway of the kitchen until most of the roaches had scurried away. Then, I would make my way to the refrigerator for a bottle. These two vivid memories were excellent motivators for me. I knew that I could not quit! Quitting was never an option.

When I returned to school, I was working full time and going to school full time. I did my required readings and reports in the morning (4 a.m. to 6:30 a.m.) before the children awoke for school. Generally, I attended classes from 8 a.m. to 12 noon and I worked from 1 p.m. until 9 p.m. I completed all of the requirements for the associate degree in African-American Studies in two semesters.

It was a very challenging year, emotionally and financially. Money was always scarce. The baby-sitter quit. Child support was sporadic during the first year and later became non-existent. My life was in complete turmoil. I had absolutely no money left over once I paid my bills and childcare. Our first Christmas after my separation, we received a donated Christmas tree from a local church. "Friends" of the adoption agency provided gifts for the children I was adopting. It was tough, but I focused on what I did have, thank God. In spite of all the challenges

I have three wonderful healthy children, a great support system and a dream for a better tomorrow.

I completed the forms for graduation and realized that I did not have enough money to pay the graduation fees. I did not participate in the graduation ceremony. I know that my father or one of my brothers would have given me the money if I had asked, but they had already given me so much. My brother Charles had saved my house from foreclosure just months before, so my children and I had a place to stay. I simply could not ask for anything more, from anyone. I quietly decided to forego graduation.

I was admitted to the University of San Francisco (USF), but I could not pay tuition. I had lost my job the month after I graduated and was dependent upon unemployment when I was accepted into a four-year school. A friend heard about my desire to attend school and my lack of funds. He quickly offered to pay the initial funds (about $1,000) so that I could begin classes. It was hard to believe the offer. I was hesitant, but he insisted that he would not miss the money. I promised to repay him. And I did!

In my second semester at USF, my guardian angel intervened again. The financial aid office sent me a notice in the mail that my tuition for the semester had been paid in full. I had inquired about a grant when I was accepted, but all funds had been committed. I had completed the paperwork anyway, and this was the payoff.

Having faith and doing your part (in this case filling out the paperwork) pays off! You cannot win if you are not in the race. I entered the race for the funds when I returned the completed paperwork, even though I had been told that no funds would be available.

I completed the course requirements for the bachelor's degree at USF in one year. I took an additional year to complete my thesis project. This time I went to graduation. It was wonderful! My parents were there. My three children were there. My ex-husband Darryl was there. The friend who provided the initial money for my education was there. It was a memorable occasion.

Initially, I had decided to go to graduation solely for my parents to have the opportunity of seeing me graduate. After all, I thought, I had not graduated from junior high or high school. I didn't attend my junior college graduation. The least I could do was to give them these few moments of pride and to give my children something to aspire toward. I realized, later, that attending the graduation was also for me. It had been a very long and difficult journey, but I had done it! Wow! I had the wonderful feeling of reaching a goal. I liked this feeling!

I began working as a counselor at Juvenile Hall before completing the requirements for my degree. I worked there for three years. After that, I was a social worker. That job provided the financial independence that I had sought.

Financially, life was wonderful. My salary had tripled from what I was making right after my divorce. I had adequate funds so that the lack of child support didn't matter. The goal of financial independence had been achieved and the threat of roaches and mice no longer haunted me daily. I could pay all of my bills and have money left over for fun and vacations.

It was great. But even though I was a good social worker, and the job was financially and emotionally rewarding, it was not a job that I wanted to perform for life. I began teaching parenting classes while still with Social Services and fell in love with interacting with adults who were eager to learn. I decided that I would pursue an academic career in higher education.

I found an excellent graduate education counseling program at USF and timed my graduation to coincide with Songhai's graduation from high school. I completed the program, as scheduled, but it was not easy. During the time that I was in graduate school, I had remarried and there were five teenagers living in my house — my three children (Songhai, Sylvia, and Sylvester); my stepchild (Nicole); and my niece (Melissa). Melissa and Songhai were pregnant during some of this time and two other stepchildren visited frequently.

With five teenagers in the house, for each day that I needed to go to school, there were reasons to stay at home. Something was always happening. Drama was a daily staple in our life's diet. Every time I thought that the worse that could happen had happened, something else would happen. With teenagers everything is serious. "Crisis" is their middle name. I decided that all problems would be handled on the days when I did not have to go to school. If a matter was not life threatening, I went to school. I had to remain focused or I would sink.

I completed graduate school with a 3.75 G.P.A., a far cry from my first year at Long Island University, and a remarkable accomplishment for someone who had left school in the ninth grade. Graduation day finally came. My family, my friends, and my first grandchild surrounded me in support of my accomplishment — an accomplishment that was once beyond my dreams. However, once I had developed a vision for graduate-level education, it all fell into place. I have since considered pursuing a Ph.D., and may do so in the future. It is not a goal at this point, but a possibility.

Currently, I am a divorced grandmother of six and very happy with how my life turned out. I am an Instructor of Psychology and Ethnic Studies at Solano Community College. I also maintain a consulting practice.

If there is a secret to success, for me, it is perseverance — hanging in there and having faith; faith in God, faith in Self, faith in Life. During my years of struggle as a single parent, my theme song became "I Will Survive." I was not satisfied with mere survival, but moreover, to surpass and exceed "survival" with "success."

Finally, my advice to teen mothers who are struggling is:

- Establish goals and a plan to achieve them.

- Write them down! Figure out in advance what motivating thoughts can be held on to when the going gets tough, and it will.

- Success requires dedication, commitment, and hard work, but the rewards are awesome.

- Become financially independent so that you do not have to depend upon someone else's choices to support your children and maintain the lifestyle of your choice.

- Be True To Yourself! After all is said and done, you must be able to live with yourself and the consequences of your decisions.

- Choose your life partner carefully. And don't settle for less in a partner than you know you deserve.

I Never Thought This Could Happen

The Antoinette Williams Story

Antoinette is a 32-year-old African-American. She is married (second husband), a mother of two (one biological son and one stepdaughter) and lives in Georgia. She is a social worker with a Master's (MSW) degree. Her mother works in medical records and her father has been in construction and owns apartments. She grew up in Miami, Florida. She has three brothers and she is a middle child.

I was trying to get pregnant and I got pregnant at nineteen. In the fourth month of my pregnancy, I started spotting, so the doctors put me on bed rest. By the sixth month, they told me that something was wrong. I was admitted to the hospital. The baby had stopped breathing. They performed a Cesarean section. My son weighed one pound and five ounces at the time of birth and there were complications from there.

After everything settled down, they explained that I had experienced pre-eclampsia. The amniotic fluid had disappeared. My water had not broken and my son had stopped growing around the fourth or fifth month. I didn't smoke. I didn't drink. I didn't abuse any type of prescription drugs. I didn't eat vegetables, but outside of that, I took my vitamins. I don't know what caused it, nor do the doctors.

Quintin is twelve now. He is attending public school in special classes. He has had long lasting health problems from being born prematurely. He has epilepsy and hypoglycemia. He needs to eat every three hours, he has asthma, and he is small for his age. He is learning at the fourth grade level. Overall, he has done well for the most part. Nightly, he is fed a special formula through a "g-tube." The tube was developed at Egleston Children's Hospital.

I was scared when I had my baby even though Quintin was a planned baby. I was a teenager who had all the answers. I had my life all planned. I was going to graduate from high school, get married, have a baby, go to college, pursue my career, and everything was going to be "hunky dory." So I graduated from high school and got pregnant. Pregnancy is supposed to be a joyous time, at least that is what I thought. Nobody had ever talked to me about what could go wrong during pregnancy. When the complications began, the doctor didn't really tell me anything. Being young, I didn't know the questions to ask or what was really happening. I didn't know how pregnancy was supposed to go. It was a scary time. My husband was young (twenty/twenty-one) at the time. I was away from family. I had moved to Rhode Island because he was in the military. No one really talked to us even after Quintin was born. He stayed in the hospital for a good four to five months.

As soon as we took him home, we had to take him back to the hospital. He began to have seizures and low blood sugar. They didn't tell us anything. It may have been because I was a young mom, but I didn't know that he was an ill child. I felt very left out. I wish I had known then the things I know today. I would have known what to ask. I would have done some things differently.

I flew home and stayed with my mom a couple of times. It seemed as if I was a single parent at times, because my husband was away at sea. Taking care of Quintin, everything fell on me. We went back and forth to the hundreds of doctors he needed to see. He has been to many children's hospitals. I divorced my husband because he couldn't handle Quintin's health problems, among other things. We now have a pediatrician who has taken the time to explain things to us. She has helped us to understand what is happening with Quintin's body.

The others had basically given up on him. I have been told that there is probably not another case in the country like his. It has been a long hard battle. I have been blamed for his development. He would not gain weight so the doctors said that his failure to thrive was my fault. After he was admitted to a hospital, they confirmed that he was not eating or gaining weight; so it wasn't me.

I survived on my faith in God and with the help of my support system. My mom was as supportive as she could be from Miami to Rhode Island. I had friends that I depended on. My grandmother provided a strong foundation as well. Through an Early Intervention Program, I had a home health person come out and show me some things to do for Quintin's development, his health, and his special needs. To maintain, I took it one day at a time.

Quintin practically lived in the hospital for the first two to three years of his life. I spent most of my time at the hospital. When I look back, I don't know how I survived. It was a really trying time. I didn't know if I would make it. I was going to counseling. I had been sexually abused and I was dealing with that. My decisions to get married and to get pregnant caused old wounds to reopen, especially after Quintin arrived with all of his medical problems.

My experiences with Quintin helped me to decide upon my career. I would either become a doctor, a lawyer or a social worker because I had encountered so many systems with him that were not as informative as I thought they should be. Becoming a doctor would have required too much time away from him. I also knew that I wouldn't be able to be a lawyer and defend anyone whom I knew to be guilty. I had dealt with a lot of social service agencies. In the military, they were not at all sympathetic to Quintin's medical condition.

Social work was a way for me to give back the good that people had given me. I wanted to change some existing systems that I felt had done some disservice to me. I went back to college a year and half after Quintin's birth. I had spent so much time looking at the four walls at the hospital. I was always expecting Quintin to die rather than to live. There was nothing I could do to facilitate his getting better, so I decided to go back to school to occupy my time. It was one of my goals and I was going to do it.

After receiving my A.A. degree in Human Services at Bristol Community College, I got my B.S. degree in Social Work from the University of West Florida. I then attended Clark-Atlanta University for my Masters in Social Work. I made it through prayer, perseverance, and positive people. The more positive people I surrounded myself with, the better things seemed to be. The more information I got regarding Quintin's health, my own health and mental well being improved and the more strength I seemed to have.

Quintin motivated me to go on. I really felt that I needed to do for him because he was my choice. I had decided to get pregnant and to bring him here. It was incumbent on me to do the best that I could for him and for me. My mother had raised me not to give up. Challenges make a person strong. This is the first time that I have talked publicly about my challenges with Quintin. It is quite emotional for me. At a recent meeting, I heard some feedback from people that they needed to hear this kind of information. A Ph.D. in Social Work is a major goal for me. I want to work for special needs children's issues to give families what they really need and to educate schools on the needs of children. We have not done enough to help.

I have met other women who have both a special needs child and another child. It has made their home lives very difficult. Quintin is pretty much self sufficient now. I am currently remarried and my husband and I are planning to have more children.

My advice to teen mothers is:

- *Be strong and have faith in the higher power.*

- *Surround yourself with positive people.*

- *Find people who will help you to build on your strengths and go on from there.*

Date Rape

The Inez Guillory Story

Inez is a 45-year-old African-American. She is married, a mother of five, and lives in Northern California. She is a Captain in the United States Air Force and holds a B.S. degree in Nursing. Her mother is retired, and her father is deceased. She grew up in Northern California, with six sisters and five brothers. She is the second oldest child.

It was a date rape. During the 60s and 70s, there was no name for it. I was going out with a guy who was 18 and I was 14. He was a member of a community organization. He was really a hero in my eyes. The organization's headquarters was down the street from where we lived. Although he made me feel special, I had no intention of having sex with the guy. It was never on my mind. We went to parties and talked about different political views. We were really excited because a lot of changes were beginning to happen. I didn't think that our relationship was going to be anything more than just going out. As it turned out, I was in a situation that got out of control.

My mom wasn't home when it happened, but my brothers and sisters were. We lived upstairs and had to climb 35 steps before entering the front door. One night, he brought me home after a party. We began kissing. I didn't anticipate a problem, but I felt uncomfortable when he began touching me everywhere. I asked him to stop, but he wouldn't. He threatened me. I didn't want to get hurt and I was afraid for my brothers and sisters. I felt like there wasn't anything I could do. I felt really helpless, so I started crying. We had sex, right there, in the hallway. When it was over, I just cried. I went upstairs to the bathroom and noticed that I was bleeding. I didn't say anything about it to anyone. I went to bed.

During my teens, I didn't like greens. Suddenly, I had a strong craving for greens. One Sunday, my mother was cooking greens with dinner and I told her that I couldn't wait for her to finish cooking so that I could eat some greens. She looked at me and asked, "What have you been doing?" All I could do was cry.

I went to a family practitioner and confirmed my pregnancy. My mother was really surprised that I was pregnant. Until now, I had been a very responsible person. I helped take care of my brothers and sisters. I always completed my chores. I had done well in school (I had a B average). I enrolled in a teen mother program at the YWCA. I continued to stay in school and delivered the first week of my sophomore year in high school. My mom helped me with my child while I was in school. She was very supportive.

I continued to go to school for a little while and then dropped out. My son was sick a lot. He had pneumonia and was hospitalized. I felt that

I needed to be home. I went to summer school and night school in addition to returning to high school. After his first year, I graduated with my senior class. I graduated with the President's Physical Fitness Award and the Most Dedicated Student Award, which made me feel really good.

Mine was a very difficult situation. The father of my child denied him. He wouldn't speak to me when I saw him on the street. It was a really humiliating, belittling, and painful experience. I thought, What did I do to deserve this kind of treatment? Here I was carrying this guy's child, while he was denying that he was the father. He wouldn't speak to me in public. He behaved like I didn't exist. I just felt really, really bad.

After the child was born, he came by my house once. He dropped off a case of milk and then left. That was it until my son was about 17 years old. We finally went to court. He admitted, after blood tests and 17 years of humiliation, that he was the father of my son.

My biggest challenge was my lack of self-confidence. The problems were sometimes overwhelming. I thought, "How am I going to college? How am I going to pay the tuition?" People have babies all the time. What I needed to do now was to focus on taking care of my children and getting my education. No one told me how to do it. No one helped me to draw up a plan. No one showed me workable options. So, through mishaps and blessings, people here and there, I heard about different programs. My friends said, "Why don't you look into this program?" It was purely by the grace of God that I was able to get into the Educational Opportunity Program (EOP). The Educational Opportunity grant helped me to pay for books and uniforms. That was my biggest concern at the time.

Initially, I began college in 1971. However, shortly thereafter, I became distracted and got married. I went to college again in 1980. I had been working as a community health worker when I was laid off my job. Well, I thought, This is an opportunity. I can enroll on welfare and return to college to work on my degree. I had to do something that would help me to become independent and self-sufficient. I enrolled at a community college in Oakland in the Licensed Vocational Nursing (LVN) Program.

After completing that program, I believed that if I could be a LVN, surely I could be a Registered Nurse (R.N.). I decided to go back to school to work on my Bachelor of Science in Nursing (B.S.N.). I married my current husband in 1984. He was in the Navy and I was working on my prerequisites. We moved to Virginia and I was accepted at Old Dominion University, where I graduated with a B.S.N. in 1988.

I had finally found the right guy. Because of what had happened to me, not fighting for myself during that time had really altered my level of strength by taking away my self-confidence. Now I will fight like hell! I don't want anyone to take advantage of me. I went through a lot before I learned to say, "No." That event really changed my whole outlook, especially how I felt about myself and what I could attain in life.

My husband was on active duty as an officer in the Navy. I followed him around the United States with our children. When I received my degree in 1988, I had four children at home. They were in elementary, junior high, and high school, while I was in college. The children were a tremendous help. I studied nursing and took general education classes at the same time. My three credit-hour Western Civilization class demanded more studying than my 10 credit-hour nursing class in terms of writing papers. Often, I would have my children help me. They would type my papers for me while I would finish up on another. It brought us closer together and it gave them a good indication of what to expect from college life. My husband would often help me, too. It became a family project and it brought us closer together.

After I graduated, we returned to California. I worked at the naval hospital until we went to Japan where I also worked at a naval hospital. When my husband retired in 1996, we moved to Texas. I told him, when he retired, I would see if I could get a commission into the Air Force. This was something I had dreamed of doing. My husband and I had discussed it several times. It was now or never.

I am about 130 pounds. When you look at me, you don't see my life's experiences. You just see a young African-American woman who looks fit, and who has a degree. People assume that I've had a wonderful life. They don't see my past. They don't see the pain, growth, and development. I told the recruiter that it was a) always my dream to be a flight nurse; b) that I wanted to work in an intensive care unit and transport critically ill newborns; c) that I was interested in fulfilling my dreams before I died; and, d) that I didn't want to live until I was 105, 75, 65, 55 or 45 without living out as many dreams as possible. Being a United States Air Force nurse was one of my dreams.

The Air Force sent newly commissioned officers to Alabama for officer's training. It was challenging, exciting, and great fun. My first duty station was Northern California, back home. It was a great assignment with so many opportunities to grow in the Air Force as well as in professional nursing. I was nominated Senior Company Grade Officer for my squadron. There were 200 to 250 officers in my squadron. It was a great honor. I was competing with officers in their twenties, who had no children.

Whereas, others may take things for granted, I did not. I really appreciated all the opportunities that the United States Air Force provided me. It was an honor to give back to my country and to my community. I will not be able to retire from the military because I can only serve for four years. Everything in life is give and take. I am giving my best and I am happy to have the opportunity to live my dream.

What motivates me is the determination to envision myself as a normal part of society and not as an outcast. I am an African-American woman and a minority in terms of my color, but I am no longer in the lower socio-economic status. I am no longer uneducated. I am no longer on welfare. I'm trying to improve myself. I want to be the best that I can be. I want to take advantage of all of the opportunities that are available to me.

My greatest blessings in life, my greatest gifts in life, my greatest joys in life have been my children. My children motivate me to keep going. I wanted a better life for them. When I attended community college, we lived in low-income housing. The multiplex we lived in was filled with many types of people. The multiplex next to us had drugs running rampant, and every six months, a black male that we had known was murdered. I thought, "Oh my God, I have to get out of here. My sons can't grow up like this."

Getting out of that environment was a major factor to my peace of mind. My children say that they would have still gone to college even if they had stayed in that area. I didn't feel that way then nor now. I felt that my sons would have suffered the same deadly consequences. We had seen other children in the neighborhood murdered. I just couldn't allow that to happen to my children. As it turns out, three have graduated from college and two have Master's degrees.

My heroines are my grandmother, Maggie McHenry, freedom fighter Harriet Tubman, and scientist Mae Jemison. My grandmother was the one who told me that getting pregnant wasn't an excuse for not accomplishing my dreams. Harriet Tubman was a civil war nurse who freed herself and her family. Mae Jemison, a former NASA astronaut, represents the future, giving me inspiration to continue dreaming.

After my commission ends with the military in 2001, I plan to work for Kaiser Hospital. I also plan to return to school to work on my Master's degree. I want to be the best parent, grandparent, nurse, and wife that I can be.

In 1995 I climbed Mt. Fuji in Japan with my 14-year-old daughter. It is 12,000 feet high. My daughter complained the whole time. It took us approximately six hours to reach the top. When we finally arrived at the top, my daughter said, "Wow! Mom, I'm really glad that we did it." Life will present you with mountains to climb. Just keep putting one foot in front of the other and keep going. Ask for support. You can do it. Know that God will help you to find a way. My advice to teen moms is:

- *Never give up. Believe that God has great plans for your lives. Believe it. Never listen to "No." Follow your heart. Don't let anyone determine who you are. Life is really what you make it.*

The Delphine Metcalf Story

Delphine is a 56-year-old African-American. She is a divorced mother of four children, and currently resides in Northern California. She retired from the U.S. Army at the rank of First Sergeant. She is also retired from the federal government as a Quality Assurance Work Leader (GS-11). She is currently the Commander for District 1 of the Disabled Veterans and a volunteer driver for veterans. She is a student at Sonoma State University.

She received her A.A. degree in Psychology in 1997. She was born in Northern California. Her parents were originally from Alabama. Her father passed away when she was seven years old. She has one sister and two brothers (one brother passed away in 1994). She is the youngest female child. Both of her parents worked for the government. Her father was a cook and he was in the Spanish American War, 9th Cavalry (all black). Her mother worked in housekeeping/nursing.

I got pregnant at age fifteen. Today, it might be a little more common to become a single parent than it was in the 50's. Today, they would call it date rape or statutory rape. It was the first time I'd ever been out with a young man. Not knowing anything about sex, I became pregnant the first time I had intercourse. I was unaware of the methods for preventing pregnancy.

I was angry with the young man. When he found out, he asked me to marry him, but I did not. My family was an upstanding family. I felt ashamed and angry. Mom was very upset.

She wanted me to drop out of school and go to a home for unwed mothers, but I begged her to let me stay in school until June.

In June, I went to a home for unwed mothers. I had my daughter there. Most of the girls there were giving up their children for adoption. I did not give my child up. She was born on September 26, 1958. I went back to my high school in October and graduated at seventeen with my two-year-old daughter attending my graduation.

As I look back at my situation, I don't know how I survived the many things I came up against. I was very determined to keep my child. My mom said that I had to do it myself. I got up at 5 a.m., took my daughter to the babysitter, and went on to school. A major challenge for me was not being accepted. People thought that I would not make it. It started the day after I had my child.

When I went back to school, a counselor told me that I should not come back to day school. She didn't believe that I could maintain my studies and my responsibilities as a mother, too. However, I was the first in my city that I can remember, to have a child and return to day school. I refused to go to night school or to drop out of school, as the counselor believed I would. I continued high school for two years and completed my studies.

I had to come home, wash my daughter's clothes, do my chores, and do my homework while all of my friends were partying and having a good time. I did not have a normal teenage life. I went to my junior and senior proms, like others, but I felt as if I was different. It was quite difficult trying to juggle both lives. A friend of the family, Mrs. Wallace, watched my daughter for my remaining two years in school — until I graduated.

There were obstacles then, but now, I look back on them as challenges. I kept telling myself: NO ONE IS GOING TO TELL ME WHAT I CANNOT DO. The more they told me that I couldn't do it, and the more I had to struggle with my daughter, the more I knew that I was going to make it. Nothing was going to stop me. I wasn't going to let anything or anyone stop me. As a matter of fact, I would get angry when people told me what I couldn't do. That, in itself, was a challenge. People expected me to fail — expected me not to make it.

If it weren't for the supportive people in my life, I would never have made it. My girlfriend, my best friend, Vivian, always lifted me up. She'd say, "Come on. We are going to do this together." She would encourage me to go on with my life. When I wanted to do something, she or my sister would watch my daughter. The people at church made me feel good when I brought my daughter to church. My neighbors began to accept me. We now call these types of people "mentors," but they were my extended family.

I got married and had my second daughter at nineteen. My son was born when I was twenty-one, and a third daughter was born four years later. At twenty-five, I moved to Berkeley and my husband and I divorced after I found out that he had been unfaithful. I had four children to support and I was working as a nursing assistant at the hospital and at a nursing registry.

Working two jobs was normal for survival, at the time. Mom had moved to Oakland and she helped me as much as she could. Just trying to survive and raise the children was a job. My mother-in-law wanted to help me out by raising my youngest daughter, which she did. I remarried at thirty-two.

I was working for the Army at the Presidio as a nursing assistant. My supervisor, Major White, an African-American female, called me to her office. I was thinking, "Oh, my God, what did I do now?" I have always been very verbal. I know that being a young mother, taking on responsibilities so young in my life made me that way. I never took a back seat and if anybody had a problem and told me, I would be right out front. I was very militant during those years. Because of my early-learned survival techniques, I would let nothing stand in my way.

Major White told me that she had always seen the determination in me to succeed. She asked me to have a seat and said, "Delphine, I can see something in you. I wanted to ask you: Have you ever thought about going into the

Army?" I was 34 years old. "Me, in the Army?" I asked. At the time, I was married and raising three children. I was somewhat militant, wearing my Afro. "Are you kidding? I can't go in any Army. Why should I go into the Army?" She said, "Well, I have been watching you for the past two years and I like the way you demand respect. You are a caring person and I see that people respect your judgment. You are a leader. I think you can really make it in the service. First of all, you are not going in there as an average female. You are not going in there because you want a husband; you're married. You are not going in there because you want a family; you have a family. You are not going in there because you need a job; you have a job. What I see you going in there for is to be a role model." "A role model?" I asked. "Yes, a role model for other females, especially African American females. I've heard a little bit about your history, and I can see that you are someone who people can look up to, and trust. When you get to be a certain age, wouldn't you like more than one retirement?" Of course, my antennae went up then. I asked, "More than one retirement?" "Yes. I'm sure that you will retire from the government. But how about another check and more security? Do you want to work until you are 60 or 70? You have possibilities; and you can do it." "No way," I laughed.

    I remember going home and telling my family. My husband said, "They must be crazy. You? How are you going to make it in the Army at thirty-four years old? You are so vocal, and I can't see someone telling you what to do. No way!" My mind automatically went back to when I was fifteen, to the same counselor who had told me that I couldn't make it; to the same counselor who had said that I should not return to school in the daytime because of my responsibilities as a mother.

I looked at my husband and my kids who were laughing at me saying, "Mom, you can't do this." I was thinking, "What do you mean, I can't?" After about three months of hearing all of the negatives from my family, I cut off my Afro and signed up.

At the time, my daughter didn't know what she wanted to do. She was working a part-time job and just about to finish high school. She didn't know if she wanted to go to college. I asked her, "Why don't you come with me?" She replied, "What? Go to basic training?" She told her friends and they thought it was a big joke. Even then, they thought it was a Girl Scout camp. They said to her, "It's only the reserves. So, how bad can it be? And, if your mom can make it, we know you can."

My daughter and I were the first mother/daughter team to go to basic training in Fort Jackson, S.C. We went together. Because we had different last names, I told her not to tell anyone that I was her mother. After three days at Ft. Jackson, I was called into the office of the Sergeant. A female and a male sergeant looked me up and down and began smiling. I was having all of these thoughts about how females are perceived in the military. I was thirty-four years old. I was not nineteen. I was thinking negatively.

They said, "We are not laughing at you. We heard that there was a mother and daughter team coming to Fort Jackson and we couldn't believe it. We said, 'No way.' All of the guys are betting that the daughter will make it and that the mother will go home in a couple of weeks. We told them that we would not bet anything until we had seen you. We have seen you. We saw you out there beating all of these young people running. We saw you doing those push-ups, and all of our money is going on you. You are going to make it here." From that day on I became the "mother figure" in basic training hearing all the problems of the soldiers in my company.

Mom made it and daughter was sent home in two weeks. I have been in the military for twenty-one years. I was in a combat zone in Desert Storm for a year and a half. I received two bronze stars and retired from the reserves in 1996. I enjoyed my military career. I was not only able to retire, but I was able to be a leader and a mentor for many young people in my military career. I had learned from my own survival techniques as a young mother. I was able to survive.

My second husband and I divorced because he wanted me to get out of the military. He was in the Navy. I looked at my life and asked myself, Did I come this far, to give it all up? I have never given up on anything that I have wanted or believed in. I decided to stay in. We divorced and I have continued to raise my children and keep my career intact.

I retired at fifty-three years of age with two retirements. For just a high school graduate, a teen mom, and someone who was not supposed to make it, I know that I have done well with the help of God and all who believed in me. I am also a grandmother of six and a great-grandmother of one. And through it all, it was always impossible for anyone to hinder me from doing what I wanted to do in my life.

It has been hard, at times. I lost my only son to drugs in 1988. I thought it to be a setback that I could not handle. You never can overcome the death of a child, but I was able to maintain. I was able to take that hard knock in my life and help other young people to understand more how life can be so short if they choose to do the wrong things. I lost my mother two months after I graduated from college. I can still see the smile on her face. I know that she was proud of the daughter who made it through.

I have been able to mentor many people as the result of my experiences. I raised my oldest grandson from the age of nine. He graduated high school in 1996 with a 3.8 GPA and is currently in college. I was able to overcome all these obstacles because I had faith. I am the first African-American female Commander of Disabled

Veterans, District 1 and one of the few who was in a combat zone in the military. I assist nine chapters of Veterans.

Many people whom I grew up with wonder how I made it: she was a single teenage parent; she lost a child; she sometimes had three jobs; she was in the war; she got her degree; and she is still going to school. It never stops. I have a dream.

My plan for the future is to earn a Ph.D. in Psychology. I am now a senior at Sonoma State University and will graduate in May, 2001 with a B.S. in Liberal Studies. I intend to work with African-Americans, especially African-American children and female veterans who have been in the combat zone as I have been. Currently, I am a mentor for two young ladies in a Vallejo (CA) Middle School and work closely with the Fighting Back Program, which provides a variety of support services to young people in the community. I have also met a wonderful man who I very much enjoy being with, after all these years. God has truly been good to me.

One of the best ways to help my comrades is by getting a higher degree. Through my lifetime, I have mentored many women who are single parents. People ask me why I need a Ph.D. They feel that I have done enough in my life without a Ph.D. I know I that have done well with the help of God, but I still have a goal.

be my motto that I wish to share with teen mothers. Don't try to move the mountain, learn how to climb it. You will be a better person once you do. In life, you will always have mountains that come your way, but you have to have faith.

Always keep God in your life and believe in yourself. Other people may not believe in you, but if you have strong convictions about yourself and who you are, as I did, you will always make it. You will not let anything "rain on your parade." No matter what kind of obstacles come your way, even if you are not doing as well as you think you should, always keep the faith and NEVER LET ANYONE TELL YOU WHAT YOU CANNOT DO.

Once you learn that life is full of ups and downs, you can climb that mountain. It will all even out one day. The mountains will turn to hills, and then turn to small speed bumps in the road. I will always believe that a child cannot be what a child cannot see. I hope to be a person whom they can see and one who can make a difference in some young person's life. I want them to realize that it is so important to have a goal in life and that the moment they stop moving toward a goal, they become the obstacle.

The High School Young Mothers Program

The Dana Littlepage Story

Dana is a 27-year-old African American. She is the mother of two children and lives in Northern California. She is a registered nurse, working in public health nursing. She is currently pursing a master's degree. Her father was in the military and her mother worked in nursing. Born in Oklahoma, she has lived all over the United States. She has five brothers and one sister (her older brother died when she was 12). She is number four in the birth order.

I was dating this guy and was obviously sexually active. No one wanted us to see each other. Granted, I was cutting school and sneaking out of the house. My brothers were not happy about the situation. My mother didn't care for my seeing this person. One way that she thought she could stop me from seeing this guy and stop me from being sexually active was to revoke my birth control pills. I wanted to be responsible, so I still got birth control pills. I had an ovarian infection and was put on medication.

No one explained to me, at the time, that antibiotics would make the pill, basically, ineffective. So, I ended up getting pregnant. I didn't realize that I was pregnant. I was frequently sick. I went to the doctor and was told that I was pregnant. My doctor tried to keep this information confidential, but my parents demanded that my records be released. I was thankful that this doctor had the courage to refuse to tell my parents and to hold my medical records until I decided what I was going to do.

My parents were not happy. They were really upset. My mother had mixed emotions. One minute, she was happy and trying to help me. The next minute, she was out to get me. Her reactions were confusing and difficult to understand. I was fifteen at the time. Sex was new to me and so was pregnancy. I had contemplated having an abortion, but a lot of time had passed. My boyfriend told me that he had some money saved and would help me, but instead he bought a car and totally forgot about the pregnancy.

My boyfriend had gotten involved with a murder and I became an accomplice, after the fact. This was someone whom I loved, so naturally, I wanted to help him. Besides, I did not want the father of my baby to go to prison for life. My actions caused me a lot of grief. My boyfriend's home and his friend's home were raided, and they were both arrested for murder.

The next day at school, an investigator from the District Attorney's office came with two officers in uniform and escorted me out of class. They said that they needed to talk to me about what I knew and my affiliation with the suspects. I was not only afraid, but I was concerned about my future and my baby's future. Here I was fifteen and in high school. We lived in a very suburban environment, so where did this violence stem from? I continued my efforts to protect my boyfriend. I talked off the record and kept my statements vague.

I was alone during my pregnancy and really did not have anyone to turn to. My parents seemed so angry because of my past behavior and the current issue that I did not have a nurturing relationship with them. My brothers and sister were too young to really understand what I was going through. They only knew that I was in trouble.

I remember being six months pregnant and feeling that the pain and the pressure were too much to bear alone. I went to the garage, found some rope, and began to plan my suicide. Just as I had completed the noose, I felt something flutter in my stomach. At first, I thought it was fear, but when I lifted my shirt, I could see my stomach actually move. At that point in my pregnancy, I realized that my baby needed me to be stronger than I had ever had to be. I recognized then that this whole thing that we call life and experience was not just about me. It was about learning what accountability and responsibility was all about. Finally, I understood that I had a positive reason for living – my baby.

I lived with my family after I had the baby. I became depressed again. I went through pregnancy and labor without positive support. The father of my baby was in jail. I had only spoken with him two to three times throughout my pregnancy. My mother did not want his family to see my baby at all. She said that I was not allowed to visit them or to communicate with them. I did not feel that way. I wanted my baby to know her paternal family. Financially, everything seemed to be a strain.

My family loved the baby, but providing for her needs became a topic for argument. I needed to support my child, so I picked up a job at a pizza place down the street. I would work and my brother or little sister would watch the baby. I wanted to buy the things that the baby needed like clothes, diapers, and milk. I also had necessities as well. My mother virtually took my money and told me that I did not need anything. She made me pay my brothers and sister for watching the baby, which was okay, but what I had to pay was ridiculous. She also made me pay some other bills. I didn't mind that either, but my needs were not being met.

My working, going to school, and getting up at night with the baby was wearing me down — not to mention, the cleaning, the cooking and the rearing of my brothers and sister. Nothing I did at home was ever good enough. I endured insults and negative comments from my father. Once again, I felt like killing myself. The stress was too much. There were too many responsibilities. It was a problem disciplining my brother and sister. My parents would say, "We don't want you touching our kids. Just take care of your own." But at the same time, there was nobody there to provide supervision for them.

My mother wanted me to give custody of the baby to them. I did not want to. I felt that they would take my baby and throw me out into the street. Because I refused, they made my life miserable. The stress of the situation became more and more difficult to deal with. I came to a crossroads between killing myself or leaving. I opted to leave. I had this baby. I needed to go ahead, leave, and do what was best for me. I went to stay with my boyfriend's parents.

My mother came over and demanded that the baby be given back to her. She revoked my work permit and she called my school, telling them to make me come back home. It hurt so bad having to leave home. I missed my little sister and brothers. I cried all the time wishing that things were different. My mother wanted to control every aspect of my life and if I disagreed, then she would use any means to try to make me comply with her wishes. I realize now that maybe she did want what was best for me, but you cannot get the best from what is wrong. This situation created a larger rift in my family.

We have experienced so much pain, struggle and strife. There is no way I can begin to share the hardships our family has endured. My older brothers were in and out of trouble and now, I am. But I was destined to be different. I was determined to make a difference.

I stayed in high school. I was able to take my baby to school with me, which was great. The only drawback was that she was ill, quite frequently, but even in the midst of that, I was able to persevere. I graduated a little bit earlier than the rest of my high school class. I was motivated to go to college by my Aunt. My boyfriend's court situation was resolved when the jury found him "Not Guilty" of murder, but "Guilty" of accessory to murder. The case was taken to an appellate court, where the DA on two counts of murder overturned it. He was basically freed due to a technicality.

Three years passed before I had my second child. I lived with the father of the child for five years, during which I withstood physical and mental abuse. I did not tell anyone because I needed the financial support that he provided. He drank excessively and smoked marijuana. He did not show the children the type of attention that they deserved from a father. I had to do everything. I would wake up at 5 a.m., begin my day — not only attending to him, but also attending to the children's needs. I would go to school all day and have to come home to cook, clean, see after the children, and study half the night while they slept. I grew discouraged and depressed. I put on weight and neglected my appearance.

One of the obstacles that I had to overcome was other adults looking down on me because I was so young, especially the people in the medical profession. My daughter had an underdeveloped lung so she was always in and out of the hospital. I had to give her the respiratory treatment and I knew what to look for. I would take her to the doctor, and tell them she was having problems breathing. They would say, "You are young. You don't know what you are talking about. You don't know how to give the baby medication, I'll show you how to do it." My friend's parents would look at me in a different light. "You are pregnant. How could you do that?" It was the stigma of having a child while young and out of wedlock that contributed to the negativity.

It was hard not having access to programs that were capable of dealing with adolescent issues. There were no programs that addressed life management (finances, emotional stresses, etc.). The community at-large really suffered from denial and refused to adequately address the woes of adolescent life — let alone teen pregnancy.

The biggest obstacle that I had to overcome dealt with my feelings of isolation, both from my family and from my community. There were strong messages sent from both counterparts about my children's bi-racial status. I had been with a white man, so my children were bi-racial, a reality that many people have had to face. So, I had the racial barrier to cross with his family and my family. It was only through going to school that I came to see racism for myself.

For the most part, I have had my children hold on to their African-American culture. That's what I am. Doing that has allowed them to think that it is okay to be a lighter variation of the color.

They, however, will not get the acceptance from the white culture, as they will from black culture. I have experienced that. We talk about their issues: "You are African-American. You are a little black boy with a white daddy. You are a little black girl with a white daddy," so that they can grasp it a lot better and get a more cohesive sense of who they are. They still keep in touch with their father. We work together for the children.

When I began school, I thought of majoring in biology, but I didn't like chemistry. I thought of sociology, but I knew that I would be hungry. So I went into nursing. Nursing was a blend of the disciplines: sociology, medicine, and business. Nursing came naturally to me. I began pursuing my education at Solano College. I did odd jobs to get nursing experience. That was rewarding.

My children's father did not want me to attend the university. He wanted me to stay at a junior college. His family has never understood the importance of education or the impact of being of color without an education. Despite comments and negative attitudes, I transferred to the University of San Francisco. My boyfriend's mother took care of the children. It was so very hard. My children would cry for me when I would leave early in the morning and I would not come home until late or not until the next day. It was difficult because I felt stress from every aspect of my existence — mentally, economically, physically and socially. I cried a lot!

In school, I remember hearing stereotypical remarks about teen moms, things like: "They are looking for love." "They do not have educated parents." "They are a part of the lower class," and so on. I looked at myself and realized that it was not at all that I was looking for love; my family is very well educated and we are a part of the middle class. People run to the ghettos and capture a poor family's plight. Without regard to social ramification, they proceed to "cinema-tize" a young girl's decision to have a child and then they globalize the situation. I feel proud to say, "I am a product of the system." After all, never let the system work you — always work the system!

The secret to my success has been determination. Have faith that you can succeed. What God has for you is for you, and nobody can take it away from you. Determination, faith, and perseverance have gotten me by. My kids have motivated me to keep going. If I had stopped, there were not very many options. I could have stopped and remained on welfare or I could continue. I wanted to be able to take care of my children and myself.

I felt the fear of failure. I received extra pressure to succeed from my family — not from my immediate family, but from my aunts and uncles. It was expected that I went to school. Whenever I talked to them, they were always asking which schools I was applying to, which schools I would go to. They pushed me to get my master's degree. No matter what others said, I was not going to fall prey to pregnancy, additional pregnancy, despair and poverty. I was not going to be in a position of being impoverished all my life.

I am returning to school for a Master's Degree in Public Policy and Administration. I am especially interested in urban policy administration. I am even toying with the concept of law school. It is hard and demanding to have to work and raise your children. A lot of the things done at my job are taken home. I am tired. I really have to drag myself out to go to a lot of activities. Sometimes I miss out on a lot of things. It's hard, but at the same time, I wouldn't trade it for anything.

Other crises in my life, like my child being sick and my family not being supportive, made life even more difficult. I was involved in legal issues with the father of my children. That was tough and embarrassing. Everyone in the county knows my last name. My brother killed somebody awhile back. Over the years, the family name has accumulated a lot of bad press. It had nothing to do with me or my sister or my other brother. However, that is our name. I have had issues with that. All of those things have come together as large obstacles in my way.

My advice to teen moms is:

- Keep your head up.

- There is a goal. Strive to reach your goal.

- Your children are most important.

- Once you get your education, everything else will fall into place.

The Michelle Wallace Story

Michelle is a 28-year-old African-American. She is a married mother of three. She works in the human resources department of a major bank. She completed three years of college as a business major. Her mother is a former social worker, currently employed as a college professor, who became a single parent when Michelle was 7 years old. She has two adopted siblings. After spending her early years as an only child, she enjoyed her siblings and the opportunity of sharing her home and life with other children.

I did not see my Dad much after the divorce. He relocated, moved frequently and lived out of the country for a while. While I was growing up, we nourished and maintained our relationship through phone calls, letters, photos, and postcards while he traveled the world. I currently enjoy a good relationship with my father.

My school years were filled with basketball games, trips to the mall and hanging out with my sister and friends, until I faced the trauma of racism and discrimination that led to my expulsion from high school. My mother's friend, who is an attorney, represented me for my expulsion case. After many hearings and appeals, my record was cleared and I was allowed to return to my high school. School, unfortunately, was never the same for me after that experience. I found it difficult to attend on a regular basis. As a result I enrolled in a home study program. A few months later at the age of 16, I found out I was pregnant with my son.

When I found out, I was shocked. "It couldn't happen to me," I thought. My child's father's family was very excited and happy for me. I recall feeling afraid and unsure. My mother was initially disappointed, but very supportive. I remember her telling me, "Whatever decision you make, I will support you." That made making a decision a whole lot easier. I was very aware of the methods for preventing pregnancy. They had been taught in sex education classes, and my mother was very open about talking about and discussing sexuality. It wasn't like there wasn't birth control available to me. In fact, the day I discovered I was pregnant, I was at the hospital to get a prescription for birth control pills. I did not marry the father of my child. Marriage was discussed, but I was underage and my mother made it clear that she would not sign for me to get married. From the very beginning he was in and out of correctional facilities. Initially, I did take my son to visit his dad frequently, but after so many trips to correctional facilities, the experience wore on me. When his father *was* out of jail, he rarely came to visit his son.

Upon the birth of my son, I entered a Young Mothers High School Program. The Young Mothers Program provided childcare, so childcare was never an issue. My son's paternal grandmother was also very willing to watch him. This provided me the flexibility to leave him with her or take him with me to school. I returned to regular high school after one semester in the Young Mothers Program and graduated on time with my class. This was a major accomplishment for me because so many people said that I would not graduate from high school.

It was important to me to graduate with my class and not to allow my pregnancy to hinder my education. I felt that my mother was very disappointed in me for becoming pregnant. However, she never focused on the pregnancy/child issue, but rather, she encouraged me to not allow the pregnancy to be the obstacle that would prevent me from pursuing and achieving my goals.

Graduating from high school was a major challenge for me. I vividly remember the response of my high school principal when I told him that I was pregnant. He told me that I would never become anything and that I would not graduate from high school. Hearing this made me more determined to accomplish whatever I chose to accomplish. My mother told me to ignore the comments of those who were not supportive. I graduated from traditional high school on time.

During my last semester in high school, I went to night school and to day school to make up the credits lost when I was expelled. I attended a community college for a year and then transferred to a four-year university. I married, while still in college, and subsequently had two more children nine years after the birth of my first child.

I have always known that I would go to college since education was always emphasized in my family. I am very grateful that I was able to continue my education. During my early college experience, I dated a man who became physically abusive to me. It took a long time and a lot of money lost for me to figure my way out of that relationship. My son witnessed some of the abuse. It was very disruptive to his life because I moved four times within a twelve-month period, basically running, ducking, and dodging my abuser. It was a very stressful time for both of us.

Looking back now, I realize that my family's support played a major role during my early parenting. I don't believe that I could have made it without the support I received. There were many people cheering me on and telling me that I could do it. Saying that I had a baby wasn't an excuse. I could still accomplish whatever I wanted to achieve. I received strong family support from my extended family, also. When I went away to school, my aunt and uncle would keep my son for the weekend to enable me to study or simply to take a break. My aunt and uncle would take my son to Boy Scouts and to church. This was a tremendous help.

My son went to daycare on campus. There was also a time when he was sick and could not attend childcare. I was in the middle of finals and the Dean opened his office to my son so that he could lie on the couch until I finished my exams. I was surrounded by people who supported me.

My mother provided a car and much needed financial support and my uncle threw in a gas credit card and some cash on the side.

As a young parent, it was difficult for me to be respected by teachers and other parents. Because I was a young mother, people thought that I wouldn't have goals, dreams, and aspirations for myself or for my child. A lack of respect was displayed simply because I was a teen mom. I stayed focused. I prayed a lot and I was determined not to allow other people to dictate to me how my life was going to turn out.

Prayer and faith have kept me going — faith in myself and in the family support I received. My son also motivated me. I remember the day that I applied for welfare. My mother supported my son and me after his birth. She was also able to obtain medical coverage for him through her job. I did not apply for welfare until I entered college. I was told, at that time, I needed to apply for welfare to qualify for financial aid, independently of my mother's income. I remember going to the welfare office, standing in line, and having to take my son with me. I remember vowing that I would never have my child in those circumstances again. A lot of times, society has certain expectations. You must be a certain way to be successful. That is not what measures success. To me, success is doing what makes you happy. I believe that you are entitled to it.

My Mom told me something that was very instrumental in accepting welfare. "Use it; don't abuse it. Use it to your advantage and move forward." Don't let small "things" limit you. Use the tools that are available to you to become successful. It is also important to give something back and to speak up for what you believe in! I volunteer at a home for teen moms. It shocked me that when it was suggested at my office that we donate to a home for teen moms at Christmas; my co-workers were not supportive of the idea. They referred to all of the stereotypes associated with teen moms and wanted their donations to go to individuals they thought were more deserving.

I have also advocated, through my job as an employee benefits associate at a major bank to have the grandchildren of employees (the children of teen moms) included in the employment benefits package. I would have had to go on welfare in high school, like some of my friends, if my mother's job had not allowed her to carry my son on her health plan. Teen mothers have become my special cause. I mentor teen moms as a result of both my positive and negative experiences.

Currently, my time is very limited and I am not able to be on site, but I donate toiletries, bathroom products, and other items to the residents of teen mother homes. I have also taken some of the moms shopping. It is very important to motivate them and to emphasize the importance of staying in school. I share with them the importance of becoming successful, not only for themselves, but also for their children.

My plans for the future are to continue my education, possibly earning a master's degree in counseling. I feel that I am a natural counselor. I enjoy listening to others and assisting them to create healthy lives for themselves. I enjoy my current job and I would also like to grow with my current company. Because my company provides full tuition reimbursement, I would like to take full advantage of the program to further my education.

My advice to teen moms is:

- *Believe in yourself even when nobody else believes in you.*

- *Set goals. Reach for something. Don't just say, "I am going to make it." What are you going to do? How are you going to make it? Have a plan and understand that you may not get there right away. It may take more than four years to finish college, but hang in there! Even without family support, set your mind on a goal and say, "I am going to do this." You can do it with or without the support of the father. Women can raise happy, healthy, strong children by themselves. They have done it for years. Just because you are a teen parent, there is nothing that says you cannot achieve whatever you dream.*

- *Most of all, love yourself.*

Babies Having Babies

The LaRahna Martin Story

LaRahna is a 27 year-old African American. She is married, the mother of four and lives in Georgia. She has a B.A. degree in business. She founded and currently operates a small, successful consulting firm that provides workshops and seminars for businesses. She is also a co-owner of an income tax preparation franchise, with her husband. She has one brother. Her mother is college educated, a registered nurse, a college counselor and a single parent.

During the summer before my first year of high school, I got pregnant. I was thirteen years old. For five months, I hid this pregnancy from my family and friends. My mother noticed it when my clothes could no longer hide my stomach and took me immediately to the doctor. The pregnancy was confirmed and an estimated due date was given. The emotions were almost consuming. I remember what seems like days of crying.

All of the options were weighed: abortion, adoption, and teen motherhood. Abortion would have probably been the most logical decision. I did not think I could live with that decision and God probably intervened because he knew the outcome of my life. At the abortion clinic, the doctors could not confirm the age of the fetus and, therefore, would not perform an abortion. They thought that the gestation was too advanced to abort.

That left the options of adoption or raising this child alone. I had no real contact with the father. Adoption seemed the likely alternative, but it was a hard decision to make. It was not until the day after the delivery of a healthy baby boy that I decided for sure what my life would be like. Even though family members offered to adopt my child, I turned them down and took my son home.

It was a struggle. I still had more than three years of high school left. Where could a 14-year-old work? How would I support this child? The support of my mother was the temporary answer. My mother and my family sacrificed. My mother worked harder to make sure that my child had diapers, food, and clothing. My grandmother came over early in the mornings so that I could catch the bus for school. My brother came home in the afternoons and babysat so that I could study.

I worked while I went to summer school. My mother would drop me off at my summer youth job where I would work the maximum hours allowed by law. I would then go to summer school, riding my bike several miles home. I paid my grandmother ten cents an hour to watch my child while I was working.

I also had the support of my church family and a small circle of friends. With that support, I was able to graduate from high school a year early in the top fifteen percent of my class. I was accepted to college and at the age of sixteen I left home. I packed up my 2 year-old son and moved sixty miles away from home to Sonoma State University. It was scary. I didn't want to go. But my mother knew what was best for me.

This was not a plan that happened overnight. I began communicating with the university almost a year before attending. I got on the list for childcare on campus. My name was at the top of the list by the time I enrolled. I applied for financial aid and welfare, using the resources that were available to me.

I did not make it on my own. There are so many people who helped me to become successful. I had a high school friend who would come to my apartment on the weekends to help me. She would help me clean the house and wash the clothes. There were a group of friends who went to a nearby community college. My son called the group, "The Boys." They would come over to baby-sit for me in exchange for dinner, so that I could study or work. My church family embraced my son and me. My extended family did the same. There is no way I that could have completed my education without them.

My mother was my biggest supporter of all. She gave me the vision to be better. My mother taught me that no matter what, you can be better. Be educated. Be a success. She also taught me that even with the negative stigmas associated with teen pregnancy, I should hold my head up high. For that I am thankful. Many times my mother did not agree with the decisions I made, but as I grew older, I learned to appreciate her support. It has been a long road getting to this point in life. I have learned a lot from life. It has not been easy. One thing is different now. I look back and understand more fully the passage in the Bible: "All things work together for good." As a scared 13 year-old, I would never have been able to say that. Now, I can say that God knew what my life would be and that it has worked out for good. Perhaps some of the good is simply sharing my story.

My advice to young women is:

- *Work hard*

- *Set goals for your life, and*

- *Keep your faith in God.*

The Angela Young Story

Angela Young is a 33-year-old of American Indian-White-Spanish descent. She is a divorced mother of three and lives in Northern California. She is an X-Ray Technologist, who has completed two years of college. Her mother was a nurse with five girls. Angela was the youngest. Her father is retired.

I was fourteen when I found out I was pregnant. I denied it. It felt like I was pregnant, but I told myself that I couldn't be. I told my boyfriend. Half-jokingly, half-seriously he said, "It's not mine. It's my brother's," and played the denial game. When I began to get sick, throwing up, I wouldn't tell my mom what was really happening. My mom took me to the doctor many times before she figured it out herself and made me take a pregnancy test. Her way of telling me that it was positive was by bringing a baby chair to the end of my bed before she left for work. That's pretty much how I found out, for sure, that I was pregnant.

I don't think I felt anything when I found out I was pregnant. At the time, it didn't seem like a big deal. When I was fourteen, it really wasn't real. I didn't feel anything. I didn't feel happy. I didn't feel sad. I was just okay. My mom was hurt. She was upset. She wanted to kill my boyfriend. She figured that it was his fault. I was aware of the methods for preventing pregnancy, but teenage boys (maybe men in general) have a way of being very convincing. I did not marry the father of my child.

Being a teen mom was lots of work. My mom and neighbors helped out. Welfare helped out financially. My mom, actually, forcefully took over the mothering role. I stayed in school while my neighbor watched my child.

The major challenge of being a teen mom was not being able to do the same things that my friends were doing. That was a big, frustrating part of being a teen mom for me. Another was my having to take care of my child while my mother was telling me what to do. That was difficult for me. I was trying to be a mother and an adult, but I was still a child. Money was an obstacle — not having enough. Childcare was a problem. Even though I had my mother, she couldn't be there all the time. I had a child care provider while I went to college. My mom helped me by not charging me much for rent and utilities. I was living with her while I was going through an X-Ray Technician program. I attended a hospital Radiology program through a Community College.

Three and a half years passed before I had my second child. I got married when my second child was almost two years old. My husband was in the Army and we were stationed in Germany. I came back, divorced him, and went to Community College for about a year. When I got out, of the X-Ray Technician program, I was fortunate enough to work at the site where I had trained, and I have been there ever since.

My key to success has been my determination — not letting anyone tell me that I couldn't do anything. Getting out of my mother's house was my biggest motivation. As soon as I graduated and got my first couple of checks, I left. It was about a month after I graduated. I was motivated by the reality of having to provide for my kids and having to pay my bills.

My plans for the future include going back to school after my daughter graduates. I don't want to put her in the same position that I was in, with my mother working a lot of overtime. Being away from home and working overtime could leave ample opportunity for my own daughter to get pregnant. Don't let anyone tell you that you can't do it. Besides, there will always be someone out there willing to help.

College Campus Baby

The Nicole Howell Story

Nicole Howell is a 26-year-old African American. She is a divorced mother of one and lives in New York. She just completed her second year of medical school. She has two older sisters, one younger brother and a younger half brother. Her parents are divorced. Her mother is a nurse and her father is retired from the military. Both parents are college educated and have graduate degrees.

The first time I became pregnant, I was sixteen years old. It was one of those situations where I was fully aware of birth control, but I chose not to use any. It wasn't as if I was "trying" to have a baby, but I wasn't taking any precautions to avoid it either. I went for a pregnancy test and found out that I was pregnant. After I told my mother the results, she automatically assumed that this had been some attempt on my part to keep my boyfriend, which couldn't have been further from the truth. About three weeks later, on Christmas day, my mother threw me out of the house because I didn't meet her at our friend's house.

I'm sure that this was the straw that had broken the camel's back. She had been under severe emotional stress in her marriage, and the fact that I was refusing to terminate the pregnancy hadn't helped. So, on Christmas Day I walked out of the house with only the clothes on my back. My boyfriend's parents refused to let me stay at their house because they were under the delusion that since I was a minor, they could go to jail for "harboring" me. I had no where to go and no one to turn to.

Both of my sisters had abandoned me, and my boyfriend was less than supportive. I ended up staying at his cousin's house during the holiday break, which was less than ideal. I probably could have moved back to my divorced and remarried father's house, but he was busy dealing with two pregnant teens already. During that time, I felt the greatest despair ever in my life. I felt so alone, abandoned, and lost. I don't know if it was the concept of self-preservation or the hand of God (probably the latter) that prevented me from throwing myself in front of a car.

After about three weeks of being displaced, my mother let me move back home. I had decided to terminate the pregnancy. I went on to finish school that year, graduating in my junior year. I applied to college and got accepted. So I left my mother's home and moved closer to my father to attend school.

I met my boyfriend the fall of my first year in college. We decided to have a child that year, but I didn't get pregnant until the beginning of my second year of college. Since we were trying to conceive a child, it wasn't a surprise. I was eighteen years old when I got pregnant. I was worried about how my mother would react, given her response the first time I had been pregnant. And now, two years later, I was pregnant again. I was really nervous about telling her that I was going to have a baby. But, when I told her, she was excited.

I have two older sisters, one almost twelve years older and one two years older. My mother had no grandchildren. She was so excited that she was going to finally have a grandchild. I told my father the same night that I found out I was pregnant. I have always maintained a close relationship with my dad. Since he lived about thirty minutes from where I went to school, I drove to his house to tell him. When I told him that I was pregnant, he said, "You sound like you are happy." I replied, "I am." My boyfriend and I got married a year after my daughter was born.

Over all, I have never looked at being a teen mom as incredibly difficult or as having caused major down time. I think that's because I have had a lot of support — not just from my family. At the time, my husband's family lived close to us. At one point, my sister-in-law, Darlene, lived in the same apartment complex. She had two children, so she would help with my daughter. In fact, when my daughter was first born, I was about to go into my third year of college.

I would take my daughter to school with me. My husband and I were both students, so it was easier to make our schedules flexible. If one of us was in class, the other one was out. If we had an overlapping of hours, we had friends who would watch our daughter for that hour. It could have been harder, but our good support system made things much easier. Besides, my daughter wasn't a difficult child. We put her in daycare when she was about 16 months old. It was near school, which allowed me to take classes and still be able to pick her up. By that time, her dad wasn't in school anymore and was working.

I can't recall any major challenges associated with being a young mother in college. I feel that I spent enough time with my child; she was not neglected in any way. There weren't any major financial issues. I was always on financial aid, and at one point, we received state assistance. As far as being a young mother, I can't think of anything that was incredibly difficult. I probably had more problems with my relationship with my husband than with being a parent.

The parenting came relatively easy, because that's something I had always wanted to do. I was very excited about becoming a parent. At this point, it is probably more difficult because she is older, her personality is fully developed and she is a lot more stubborn. When we were younger, I had momentary crises like not having a babysitter when I needed one. But then I would have to be flexible and just change my plans. In retrospect, it might appear that I am sugar coating my situation, but I didn't really ever have any major problems.

While in school, I had heard from friends that some people in school thought that I wasn't going to be a doctor because I had had a child. I have always wanted to be a doctor – from the time that I was about four. There probably were a lot of people who thought that I would not continue toward fulfilling my dreams. However, if I have my mind set on doing something, I am going to do it. I wanted to have a baby, so I had a baby. People would ask, "Why make your life so much more difficult?"

Actually, having a child has helped me to focus more. My time was more limited. I didn't have time to mess around. I had to take care of business. In fact, my grades improved because I became more organized with my time. When I sat down to study, I studied. I didn't do it halfway. I can't say that I wish I had waited to become a parent. Nor can I say that I wish I had my youth back, because I really didn't stop living my life because I had my daughter. If I needed to go out, I would get a babysitter and go out. I would take her everywhere I went, if I could. Not everybody can be a young parent. In all respects, I am not that impressed with myself. But this is what I wanted to do.

I am currently attending Medical College. My daughter, Amani, is entering the third grade. I recently gave birth to my second child as a single parent. The secret to my success has been self-motivation. I know what I want, and I know that despite any obstacles, I am going to accomplish my goals. When I first applied to medical school, I didn't get in. But I viewed it as a temporary setback, a minor obstacle, another challenge. Instead of giving up on getting into medical school, I enrolled in a post baccalaureate program to take additional courses to get into medical school. Instead of taking four years to get into medical school, it took me seven. Another critical part of my success is allowing people to help me. I've never been ashamed to ask for help, nor have I turned it down when it was offered to me.

The summer before I began medical school, I was in a bind because Amani was supposed to visit with her father in California while I attended a summer program. Due to a lack of planning on his part, I was left with the responsibility of finding a summer camp or some day activity where she could go while I was in school. The local day camp was filled. Being new to the area, I didn't know of any alternatives.

While sitting in the Minority Affairs Office on campus, I began to cry about the situation. One of the women in the office overheard me. I told her what was happening. Being a resident of the next town, she knew about a program in her area that I could afford. She further extended herself by offering me the use of her address so that I could get resident rates. Needless to say, I took her up on her offer. At the time she was a complete stranger.

My plans for the future are to complete medical school, to become a doctor, and to have more kids. Right now, I would like to be a Neonatalogist, taking care of sick newborns or to work with cancer patients. I may get interested in something else in the future. Who knows? I believe that it is important to have goals for oneself. No matter how hard it gets, no matter how difficult it seems, keep pursuing whatever you want to do. Keep in mind that there is a light at the end of the tunnel.

Also remember that there is support out there if you look for it (or cry for it). Whether they are your friends, your family, your church group or strangers; there is support. Don't feel bad about asking for help and using that support. Don't abuse it, but don't feel bad about using it. You can't survive on your own and succeed. Being a single mom or a young mom, you definitely can't survive on your own. But it is also very important to have goals set for yourself as well as to get your education. Don't let anybody tell you that you can't do something because you had a child at a young age. It just means that you got a jump-start on being a great parent.

The Ramona Garrett Story

Ramona is a 47-year-old African-American. She is a married mother of one and lives in Northern California. She holds a Juris Doctor degree and is a Superior Court Judge. Her father was in the Air Force and her mother was a homemaker. She moved to Solano County at age fourteen. She has five siblings and she is the second oldest.

While my parents were watching television, I told them that I was pregnant. They continued to watch the television and said, "That's fine, Dear. Now move out of the way. You are blocking the TV set." I was seventeen. I went to the doctor because I was experiencing nausea and I found out for sure. I was in high school, at the time, and unaware of the methods for preventing pregnancy. I was frightened.

I did not marry the father of the child and I stayed in high school until January of my senior year, when I started showing. The school had a policy that a pregnant girl who had started to show could not come back to school. So, I stayed home. I had enough credits to graduate, by that point, and I had been accepted to college. I awaited the birth of my daughter, which took place in June. In September, I took her, moved to San Jose, and started college.

During my first year, anybody whom I could find watched my daughter while I went to my classes. I didn't know much about setting up day care. I was only eighteen years old. Her father was living with me, in the beginning, and he watched her sometimes. After a while, they set up a day care center on campus for students who had children, so she went there for a while. In my second year, there were private day care centers that I had discovered and I took her there. During final exams, I took my daughter to my parents' house to stay for brief periods of time. Since we lived so far away from each other, there wasn't a whole lot that they were able to do to help.

The greatest challenge of being a teen mom, for me, was trying to figure out life and how to be a mother at the same time. It wasn't as though I had time to think about it, to reflect, and to discuss the proper way to be a mother with other people. So I had to make it up as I went along. Also, there were severe financial problems, because I was on welfare when I was in college. I received financial aid loans and scholarships, but there were times when the money would just run out before more money was coming in. It was difficult to manage.

Going to college was a painful experience for me. It was the first time that I had been away from home. I had done well in elementary and junior high without ever having to try. In high school, I was able to do fairly well without having to put forth a lot of effort. I had some really good teachers and counselors and they encouraged me. But I didn't have good study habits. I didn't know about doing research. I got through school without having to do all of that.

When I got to college, it was very different. Without study skills at Santa Clara University, which is a very well known Jesuit school, I was struggling academically. On top of that, I had a child. Financially, Santa Clara was a fairly wealthy school and I was a welfare mother during a period of major social upheaval. Between 1970 and 1974, the anti-war movement was on college campuses, including my own. Angela Davis was being tried down the street in the San Jose Superior Court. There were a lot of demonstrations and a lot of issues in the air. I felt out of place at Santa Clara.

The experience was awkward and lonely for me. But in retrospect, it was also an extraordinarily broadening and educational four years for me. I majored in philosophy, so I spent my years studying how well-know thinkers had grappled with some of the great problems of life. I enjoyed my major tremendously, and I still read philosophy books in my spare time.

I received my first exposure to the arts at Santa Clara. I studied ballet for the first time at the ripe old age of eighteen. My ballet teacher, Diana Morgan Welch, was a fan of choreographer, Martha Graham. We watched videos of Graham's dance creations. We studied sets and sculptures by Isamu Noguchi. I heard Tchaikovsky for the first time in ballet class. I first heard the name, Judith Jamison, in Diana's class.

Occasionally, I set foot in the DeSaisset Art Museum at the school. I studied voice for one semester and was introduced to operatic singing. At Santa Clara University, I debated the death penalty and abortion in a class with other students. We studied religion, ethics, and a host of other subjects that have informed and influenced my views to this day. My four years at Santa Clara provided me with both a solid liberal arts education and a strong vein of independence and self-confidence, despite the ambivalence I had felt about being there.

After college, I held a series of jobs because I didn't really know what I wanted to do. My first job was selling subscriptions for a cable television company. With that job, I was able to get off welfare. I was a sales representative, going door to door, selling cable TV subscriptions. I worked in that position until I decided to go to law school. I made that decision because I became very interested in business while working in cable television. It was my first exposure to the business world, in depth.

During that time, some members of my family were experiencing legal problems. They had come to me seeking advice. Because I was the first person to complete college in my family, people thought that I could help. It was very frustrating when I could not. That's when I entertained the idea of going to law school. I began law school in 1977, when I was 25 years old. In contrast to my undergraduate experience, law school was just wonderful. I absolutely loved law school. I attended the UC Davis School of Law, a small school. The staff was very supportive of students. It was one of the most exciting things I have ever done.

My first year, I lived in Davis. My daughter, by this time, was in elementary school. I just needed people to watch her when she finished school until I got home. Law school classes were pretty flexible. While I studied for the bar, my daughter lived with my mother. Once I passed the bar, we were reunited. I went into private practice for two years. Afterwards, I became a prosecutor in Contra Costa County. Then, I moved back to Solano County and became a prosecutor in the District Attorney's Office. I was promoted to Chief Deputy District Attorney for Solano County, where I handled a fairly high-profile murder case that took a lot of my time and attention.

A few years later, I applied for a judgeship. I believed that I could make a contribution to the community by becoming a judge, a public servant. Once I decided that I wanted to be a judge, I went for it. Governor Pete Wilson appointed me to the Municipal Court of Solano County in 1992. I am currently a Superior Court Judge.

One of the things that I have always appreciated about my family and friends is that people have left me alone. There were six kids in my family, and my parents were really busy trying to raise us. As a result, I was never told what

I could or could not do because of my gender or race by my parents. I was always an inquisitive child. I loved to read. I had a wild imagination. I became as autonomous as I could, as early as I could.

My first job was babysitting, when I was about eleven. I worked until I went to college. I have always had a lot of initiative. I was lucky enough to not have anybody kill my spirit. Whatever I imagined, I went after. There were no "nay sayers." However, obstacles pop up everyday. Some of them are small; some of them are major. It has always been my philosophy to deal with each obstacle as it comes along. I try to be productive and to keep moving forward. There has been nothing that has been so overwhelming that I thought of giving up. I have always viewed obstacles as challenges. I have always been a fighter. My motivation level has been the same, all along.

One of my life's philosophies is that one must always deal with life truthfully. You have to perceive life as clearly as possible, so that you don't entertain delusions. When you have ambitions, make sure that they are realistic. Whatever talents and limitations you have, go after the things that are within your reach. If there are problems, be honest with yourself about what your problems are and try to correct them.

Whenever I talk to teenaged mothers, I tell them that their current situation is not the end of the world. It is possible for them to achieve the things that they want out of life as long as they work hard. It sounds so cliché, but it is true as long as they are willing to work hard, complete their education, and prepare to work. Their primary responsibility is to take care of their children. By taking care of their children, by doing the things that they need to do academically, and by working wisely, all things are possible. It is good to be exposed to other people who are involved in their areas of interest. I recall hearing a lawyer speak, after I got out of college. I had never seen a lawyer before. When I heard that person, I was very impressed. I thought, I should consider law as a career. The more different types of people kids are exposed to, the more their minds are opened to the possibilities of being able to do such things, too. They can begin to dream about those things for themselves. They should not be discouraged because of their circumstances. Given the number of persons who have achieved as I have, success is quite possible.

Another crucial piece of advice to teenaged mothers is:

- Read everything that you can get your hands on. Read books, read newspapers, read magazines. There is so much in life that you will never be personally able to experience; however, many things can be experienced by reading what other people have written about. A mind can be opened tremendously. There are so many possibilities out there. The more you read, the better you get at reading. Through reading, you can begin to think more clearly. Reading is one of the main contributors to my success.

- Always place your priorities in order. Relationships with young men are important, but you have the responsibility for getting yourself together, first. A woman can not expect a relationship with a young man to complete her. She needs to prepare to do what she can on her own, so that when a young man comes along, he will want to join her from a position of strength and pride – pride in what she has been able to achieve on her own.

Songs in the Key of Life

The Karen Garcia Story

Karen is a 25-year-old Latina. She is a married mother of one and lives in Southern California. She is a CCS Technician with an Associate degree in Liberal Arts. Her stepfather worked as a foreman and her mother worked as a dental assistant, bus driver, and had a number of other jobs. Karen was raised in both California and Florida. She has three younger brothers and a younger sister.

The day is etched in my mind forever. They told me that my pregnancy test was positive. I was with my boyfriend, at the time. It didn't seem real. I was in denial that it had really even happened even though I had all the symptoms. We had dated for about a year and were sexually active.

We had used different types of birth control. We had both gone to a public health center to get the pregnancy test, and it came out positively. At that time, he was very supportive of me. Then, he got scared and sort of backed off. He went through a little period of withdrawal.

When I found out I was pregnant, I was fifteen. He was seventeen. I didn't tell my stepfather because we didn't have a good relationship. I remember not wanting to tell my mom. I kept putting it off and putting it off. My mom had given birth to me at fifteen. She was always giving me lectures about how hard it was to be a teenaged mom and all that she had to go through. I was afraid I had really disappointed her. I was scared to have to tell her. When I finally told her, she cried and walked out.

We didn't talk for months after that. It didn't make matters any easier that my mom was pregnant at that time, also. My sister and my son were born a month apart. It was especially hard because my mom was going through her own pregnancy. So, I went through the whole thing by myself with no support. I was in junior high when I got pregnant. I was supposed to start high school. I got really depressed. I wouldn't do anything but stay in my room. My girlfriends would come by to try to pick up my spirits and get me to go out. My school principal tried to get me to a school for pregnant girls. I did go for a couple of months and then I stopped. I dropped everything. I did absolutely nothing.

There was so much tension at home that I ended up leaving. I lived at my boyfriend's house. His mom had a fit. She didn't feel that it was right for me to be there, because I was just a kid and so was her son. My mom tried to get me to come back home. After having some problems at my boyfriend's house, I ended up going back home. I stayed home for two weeks. I couldn't take it any more, so I left again. After I left home for the second time, I never went back. I ended up back at my boyfriend's house and now we have been married for eight years. We lived with his folks for a while, then we moved out to our own place.

I was good in school. My mom kept repeating the importance of school but I wasn't listening. My husband and I started going to church. It wasn't until then that I decided to go back to school. The pastor there played a great role in motivating me to go back to school. At 17, I had no job, no skills, and no education. The pastor needed a secretary and hired me to work for a couple of hours a day. He really believed that there was something special in me.

I began to slack off. If I didn't feel like going to work, I wouldn't go. But my pastor was there. He was consistent. He really motivated me and helped me to regain my self-esteem. We never talked about the pregnancy. We talked about me, not what I had done. He believed in me. He gave me a chance. I felt like I really had to do something more with my life. He would constantly talk to me about school and about doing better. I ended up eventually going back to school.

Initially, I began taking classes for my GED. That wasn't working out, so I studied on my own. I just got the book and I studied. I decided to take my test. My attitude was if failed, I would try again. I'd take my chances. I would not quit. I took my test. I waited to hear the results. The letter came and I passed! It felt so good. I hadn't even been to high school. I had done it! I wasn't going to let anybody or anything make me feel badly about not having gone to high school.

With my GED, I began working at K-Mart and I went to Valley College. I chose nursing because of all the pressures from my family to be a nurse. I was doing something that people were telling me to do and it was hard. I wasn't going full time because I had to work. I was trying to balance, at a very young age, being married, raising a kid, and going to school. I took a class or two at a time. There were times when I got really discouraged because it was taking so long. But I had chosen to get pregnant. I couldn't give up. There were moments when it felt like it was taking forever. I just kept going.

I couldn't decide what I wanted to do. I had taken all of these classes to be a nurse, but I knew that in twenty years, I would not be happy. So I totally dropped nursing. It was not making me happy. It wasn't about the money. I wanted to do something where I could give back and use what I had been through. A lot of people were upset with me, but I had to do what would make me happy. When I looked at the courses that I had taken, I was qualified for a degree in liberal arts. I got a job with a County Mental Health Agency. I have been doing case management for two years. I am currently working on my B.A. degree in Sociology and Psychology.

A challenge for me was not giving up on myself; not feeling that because I hadn't done everything by the book, my chance was gone. I've felt discouraged because I didn't do everything right like finishing school, getting married, and then having a kid. I had the kid before the marriage and before school. I was not able to enjoy my youth, which was such a short period of time between being a teenager, and then a mom. I never had the opportunity to grow as a woman. I was growing up and raising a kid at the same time. I was a child raising a child.

Another obstacle, for me, was my negative self-image. The family, not just the immediate family, but extended family members looked down at me. I had just disappointed everybody. That was really hard. I was the only one of my cousins who had gotten pregnant at such a young age. I was looked at as if I was a failure, not going to do anything. Even though they never said it to my face, I knew. Instead of trying to encourage, instead of saying something positive, it seemed as if a lot of negativity came from them.

If I had listened to them, I would have become more discouraged. Instead, I became more determined. I wasn't going to end up with three or four kids. I had made one mistake, and I had learned from it. Even so, there are a lot of things that I wish had been different. Through it all, I knew that I had to be grateful, even for the hard things. It all worked out in the end. Because of my experiences, I am a stronger person today. I am amazed. I know that only God gave me a sound mind through all those years.

God is the only one who can give you a sound mind when everything around you is falling apart, when everything around you is negative. I didn't begin listening to God until I went back to church. God will take you in where you are, but he loves you too much to leave you where you are. You have to move forward.

I have felt discouraged because it seemed to have taken so long. Now, about ten years later we are buying a house, I have a nice car, I have a husband, I have a kid, and I am no longer on welfare. I have a lot to be thankful for. Although it is hard to balance, I can't neglect my child to finish my education and I have to keep my marriage together. I have to balance all of that. I can't give up.

My plans for the future are to get my Master's degree in Sociology and to work with pregnant and teenaged girls. I want to motivate them and to teach seminars for young girls. My advice to teen moms is:

- Don't give up.

- Don't give in to negativity.

- Don't limit yourself. With God, all things are possible. God can turn something bad to something wonderful in the end.

- Keep your head up.

- Know that there is always tomorrow. You can't change yesterday, but you can definitely change tomorrow.

The Linda MacFall Story

Linda is a 37-year-old Caucasian. She is a married mother of two children and lives in Northern California. She also has three stepchildren. Certified as a domestic violence and sexual assault counselor and victim's advocate, she is a crisis intervention manager. She is also a certified professional roller skating instructor and a real estate sales person.

She has completed high school and some college. Her parents married at sixteen and divorced when Linda was five. Raised in Arkansas and California, Her father was a police officer and her mother was a Licensed Vocational Nurse. As the second oldest, she has one brother and three sisters.

    I grew up poor when my mother moved my siblings and I to Arkansas, after the divorce. Mom didn't have a job, at first, so we were on welfare. My dad had been injured in an automobile accident that resulted in his being in a body cast for two years. He was unable to pay child support, so social security paid my mom three hundred dollars a month. We grew up in a very old house that, at times, had no water or heat. We grew the food that we ate. We worked very hard in our garden every day.

    At sixteen, I moved to California to live with my dad and to go to college. I had difficulties with my father and stepsister and moved out of my dad's home shortly before my eighteenth birthday. I moved in with my skating partner. We fell in love and at eighteen, I became pregnant. He was the only person in my life who had shown me much love, attention, and affection. We got married two months after our baby girl was born.

When I first discovered I was pregnant, I was very upset. I wanted an abortion. My soon-to-be-husband insisted that we have the baby. I wasn't ready to be a mother. I had five scholarships for college because I had made good grades. I had always wanted to be a pediatrician. I had planned on attending college, but due to the pregnancy that dream had vanished.

When my daughter was born, I loved being a mother. We had enough money, but our life wasn't glamorous. All of our furniture was purchased at second-hand stores and we were renting a small apartment. I wanted more. I didn't want to live in poverty any longer. I went to work at my father's real estate office. He really pushed me toward doing something with my life. He encouraged me to continue my education. He was making a lot of money selling real estate, so I thought that I would get my license and give it a try.

I worked as his secretary and attended real estate school at night. Two nights a week, I attended real estate classes at Solano College. Working daily and attending school at night was very difficult. I was only making five dollars an hour, and I had to pay two dollars an hour for day care. When I got my real estate license, I was paid on commission, only. I had to spend my own money for cards, supplies, and advertising.

While I was getting started, I couldn't afford day care, so I pushed the baby stroller from door to door. I convinced homeowners to list their homes with me. I was successful. During my first year in real estate, I listed 14 homes in my market area. It was very hard getting up early every day, getting the baby dressed, and fed; not to mention the house cleaning, cooking, and laundry. When I had to show a house, I had to beg friends to baby-sit for me.

The biggest impact of having a child so young was that I never got to have fun. I never got to party or go out with friends. I never got to go out to bars when I was twenty-one. I didn't get to because I was a mom with responsibilities. I was always tired physically and emotionally. I wanted my child to have the things in life that I never had. I had to get out and work to accomplish that. I felt guilty when I left my child at day care.

Four years after my daughter was born, I gave birth to a son. I had wanted my children to be one year apart, but I had difficulty carrying them to term. I had five miscarriages, then finally, a healthy son. Everything that I have attained in my life, thus far, has been with only my husband's support. It was a struggle to get ahead in this life without a college degree. If I could do things differently, I would have waited four years before becoming a mother. I would have gone to college and become a pediatrician. I know that I could have been much more than I am now.

Currently, my children are fifteen and nineteen. I feel that I am too old to go back to school to make my dream a reality. I make pretty good money at what I am doing now, but I feel as if I didn't develop myself to the fullest potential. I chose to throw that away and have a child. I love my children, dearly, and I love being a mother. It would have been easier if I had been more mature and financially sound. I am happy that I married my husband. We are now in our nineteenth year of marriage. Life is good.

I have spent my entire life trying to overcome the fact that I grew up in poverty. I have tried to prove myself to others and to myself. Coming from poverty, I've always felt that I was less than everyone else. I have since become more comfortable with myself. Everything I have touched, I have done very well. I am proud of myself. During those tough times, I had to keep going. I had no choice. It was either sink or swim.

My worst nightmare was that I would end up on welfare like when I was a child. Once I had children, I didn't have a choice. If I didn't want to be on welfare, I had to get out and make something of myself. I had to be an example for my children. I didn't want the cycle of poverty to carry over into their lives. I grew up with a mom who was divorced and who had five children. She had a very difficult time making ends meet.

I am working toward my retirement. My husband and I have purchased ten acres of land on a mountain in Arkansas. We plan on selling everything here in California and going back to where my family lives. We want to live in the country and to build our dream home. We have a five-year plan. We are financially set. We have a beautiful, large home with a pool. We have everything that we have ever wanted and we have worked hard for it.

My advice to teen moms is:

- Get an education. Take whatever classes you can. One way to get in the door is to volunteer for an organization. You can meet people and get job leads by networking.

- Get any little degree or certificate you can get. Start resume building. Even if you have to work on your degree little by little at night, do it. (My older sister just got her A.A. degree at age 39 and she has four kids!)

In spite of having children at a young age, a woman can grow up to be successful. She can come from nothing and still attain success. It takes commitment and hard work. And finally, there is something positive about having children at a young age…I'm still young and my children are almost grown!

Mother and Daughter Happily Ever After

This chapter looks at two teenage marriages that have beaten the odds, at least, until today. In marriages, especially in teen marriages, the partners tend to take one day at a time, thanking God for the privilege of sharing life with one another. Teen marriages are often doomed from the beginning.

The union can leave two young people trapped in a whirlwind of unforeseen struggles, major decisions, and facing the reality that "love" does not conquer all. Added to teen marriages is the premature pregnancy of an unplanned child, which further complicates an already challenging situation.

These two stories are not just examples of teen marriages, but they also depict a mother and daughter who were both teen mothers, who made the decision to marry the fathers of their children. Statistics reveal that the daughters of mothers who were teen mothers, themselves, often become victims of this same syndrome. Many times, both mother and daughter are prone to lower educational achievement and poverty. In these cases, both mother and daughter have beaten the odds of surviving teenage marriages and both have attained a high-level of education.

Vivian and Ella's stories prove that statistics are not the final determining factors, but rather, that committed individuals with vision and dreams can reach beyond traditional expectations.

The Vivian Hazzard Story

Vivian is a 35-year-old African-American. She is a married mother of two. A native of Northern, California, she currently lives in Georgia. Vivian graduated from Loma Linda University with a B.S. degree in Nursing and a Public Health Nursing (PHN) Certification. She is a Nursing Clinical Specialist, managing school-based health care centers for a major University Department of Pediatrics. Her mother is a counselor with a Ph.D. in Education and her father is a retired worker and trustee at the C&H Sugar Refinery. She has a younger brother and sister.

Several of my friends from high school began their college careers at Sacramento State, my boyfriend included. He had been there a year before me. I had graduated in the mid-semester of my senior year of high school, and in my mind I was ready for the world. I was actually very bored with the routine of home life and the constraints I felt that it had on my freedom.

I decided to leave home, go to Sacramento, and get ready for my life as a college student. I know now that this was not my only motivation. I wanted to be closer to my boyfriend and "spread my wings." The months that followed were pretty rocky. I was experiencing so many new things and learning to adjust to life. Greg, my boyfriend, had an apartment where I stayed while he was away in the hills of Humboldt County, fighting fires for the summer.

That summer left me, not closer to him, but alone, naïve, and confused. Our relationship began to fail because of my immaturity and broken trust. When the fall semester began, I had already arranged to room with girlfriends from home, who were coming to Sacramento State. Later in the year, Greg and I went our separate ways. We always seemed to keep each other at arm's length.

In December of 1980, I knew that I was pregnant. I was usually very regular with my menses, so I was sure that I was pregnant. Greg and I didn't talk about it much, we just went together to the health center to get the facts. I took the test and we returned together to get the results. We looked at each other after hearing the results as if to say, "Okay, we knew this, now what are we going to do?"

My first reaction was to get it together in my head. I was going to be a mother. I felt in my heart that we could do this because at least we had had a relationship and still loved one another. We still had to inform our parents. Not living at home made it somewhat easier. I knew that both sets of parents would be disappointed. We were both the eldest children. We were to set the example for our siblings. I felt ashamed and embarrassed. It was nerve wracking to anticipate telling our parents. When I told my parents, Greg was with me.

I will never forget it. We were sitting in the den at my parents' home. They probably knew that something was up before we told them. I remember my dad's response most clearly. He was visibly hurt. I think it was that "father/daughter/princess thing." Through the pain and hurt they were experiencing, I could still detect genuine unconditional love and acceptance of me, their daughter.

I don't remember any harsh words or destructive behavior. No shotgun was held to Greg's head. It was clear, probably more nonverbally than verbally, that we were expected to behave and make decisions from this point on as adults. As the days went on, I was going over in my head how I was going to do this, how I was going to manage. We were only seventeen and eighteen.

I had never thought about a termination seriously, but it was a topic that came up as different people talked to me. I talked to a lot of people who suggested a number of options. After talking to our parents and a health counselor, I had entertained the concept of termination. I was thinking, "What if I let all of these people down? Maybe Greg really doesn't want to be a father. Maybe he doubts that the baby is even his. I know that I have to go to school."

Greg and I talked about all of the options including termination. I had to make a decision and I decided not to terminate the pregnancy. My decision was made partially because of

Greg's willingness to be responsible and also because of the spiritual ramifications. I would have really struggled. Termination was not something that I could handle emotionally.

I never anticipated what was ahead. For the most part, I was in a daze. I was going through the motions, but truly, I was not prepared. The independent young woman who was ready to "spread her wings" had made some choices that had emotionally spread her too thin. We had talked about getting married, but we didn't want to do anything else that we weren't ready for. We waited six months or so after our son's birth to get married.

Gregory, Jr. was born on August 4th and school began at the end of August. I began that semester four to five weeks, postpartum, with Gregory attached to me in a "baby snuggly." He went to most classes with me. Very few professors objected. I had one English professor who would even hold and rock him during class since we did quite a bit of essay writing and taking tests. Eventually, I was able to get him into childcare on campus. I went back and forth, nursing him during breaks and at lunchtime.

In Sacramento, we were living one and one-half hours from our families. All of our friends, except one, were college students with no children. During the week, it was just my husband and me. We had support from our friends. My best friend was there. They made a good support system. We studied together, we went to the park, and we hung out. I didn't leave the baby often because I was nursing. Even though they did not have children at the time, our friends didn't seem to mind being around us. We were all around the same age, so they didn't have much more wisdom than we did. They were great friends and they were great for emotional support. I thank God for good friends.

The challenges that I faced were those that I had chosen to have. My greatest challenge was being a mother, a wife, and a student. Juggling all of these things along with financial obligations was stressful, many days. I realize that I was blessed. My parents and his parents were also very supportive. My parents did not turn away from me. They continued to parent. Greg's parents are in the ministry. I am sure that it was very difficult for them, but they continued to love. That really made the difference for us.

Support is really a critical issue. For the teens with whom I have worked, support seems to be the thing that makes or breaks them. Can they go home when they don't have food at their place? Can they call on their parents when they need a break? Have the parents turned their backs due to their inability to deal with the situation or due to their inability to forgive? Do they believe that they should allow the teen to suffer through a situation to extreme points to teach a lesson in "tough love?"

I wanted to go to Nursing School. At that time, the program at Sacramento State was filled. With encouragement from my husband, parents, and friends, I began to search for a school. I was accepted at Loma Linda University in Southern California. We packed our belongings and all we could stuff into our little Ford Pinto wagon. It was a very challenging time in my life.

First of all, when we arrived in Southern California, we had no place to live. The closest relative to the college was an hour's drive. We stayed with my uncle and aunt and commuted back and forth for several months. While we were commuting, I would get out of school before Greg finished at work. I would go to a very dear friend's house and wait for Greg. She would help me with the baby and with my algebra homework.

We finally located a place close to the campus. The place that we found was not on the bus line, and our little Pinto wagon was often broken. I had to walk a mile with the baby to the bus stop early in the morning to catch the bus to school. He was two years old and I would carry him along with my books and his baby bag. At times, my husband also had to walk. To save money, he would sometimes walk all the way to work, no matter the weather, about three miles. We used to joke about how the dogs would bark and chase him to work in the mornings. The joking kept us from breaking down under the stress and strain of living without a car and other items that we had taken for granted. After five years, I graduated from the Loma Linda School of Nursing. Two weeks before my graduation, I delivered my second son, Marcus.

We decided to expand our horizons. We had both been born and raised in California and wanted to provide our children with a variety of experiences and environments. In addition, my husband was interested in pursuing medical school enrollment. There were a couple of schools where he wanted to sit on their doorsteps. We moved to Georgia where we waited to hear from a school.

At seventeen, I wasn't really a spiritual person, but after Gregory was born, I felt a strong desire to do something concrete and deep with my life. Staying spiritually grounded would give me something I could hold on to, giving me a foundation of faith. A lot of people talk about having inner strength, but something has to be put there for a person to have inner strength. From a Christian perspective, for me, that is Christ. He has to be at the center of my life to create inner strength. I know that I can do all things through him.

My grandmother, "Ya-Ya," would always tell us, "Think High and Walk Tall." I know that she was disappointed when I got pregnant, but she continued to love me. She called me her "little nurse." She played a vital role in encouraging me. She was ill, but alert, when Gregory was born, and she is still an inspiration to me.

All of these things really gave me the kind of motivation that I had then and continue to have today.

Having supportive parents is crucial. Thinking from a parent's perspective, no matter what your children do or how far they go, they are a part of you. Parents never let go physically or emotionally. Other family members and close friends are also helpful. I remember that my uncles, aunts, cousins, and friends were very supportive and loving. They took active parts in counseling with me, as well as in just listening to me.

Teen parents need to be encouraged not to burn their bridges, to keep the lines of communication open. It may get very rocky. It may look like there is no way out. It may even seem as though parents have turned their backs. Parents always want the best for their children. However, parents may require time and space to accept the fact that the ideals that they set forth for their children have been altered by their children, who have chosen their own paths.

Don't give up through the storm. It is truly a storm when a parent finds out that their daughter is pregnant. Wait out the storm. Reflect on how the eagle deals with storms. The eagle flies high above the clouds, above the storm. Do that in your mind and in your spirit. Rise high above that cloud until the storm dies down. Only then can you face situations more clearly. Avoid acting rashly, in haste, in anger or fear.

A commitment to my children has also motivated me. Once I had children, I was motivated to do for them. They did not ask to be here, so I tried my best to make life pleasant for them. I feel as parents, we owe it to our children to do the best for them. That thought sustains me. I need to do certain things for myself, yet be considerate of the people left behind me. I considered my little sister and brother even when I made the decision to have my first child.

My sister was confused, I'm sure. I don't think she even knew the magnitude of the situation. The fact that I left for college was traumatic enough for her, and then, there I was stirring up stuff at the house by getting pregnant! Younger siblings don't always understand all of what is going on. For me, I needed to prove that things were going to be okay. I talk to young people all of the time and they often comment, "You and your husband made it." But for the grace of God and many people praying for us and being supportive, things could have turned out much differently. Not everyone has the benefits of our luxury.

I was recently accepted into a Nurse Practitioner Program to pursue a Master's degree in Nursing and a Nurse Practitioner license. I would like to pursue a Ph.D. and to teach nursing, at some point. Currently, I manage school-based health centers in a high-risk, inner city elementary and middle school for a major University Department of Pediatrics.

As a part of my nursing career, I managed a case group of forty teen mothers. I found myself totally committed to this work. It afforded me an opportunity to extend myself and to use my experiences to encourage them. I assisted them in making plans for themselves, not getting caught up in what is happening to them at the moment, but pressing on toward the mark. My advice to teen moms is:

- Don't be crisis oriented. Move away from a crisis. Envision what you want for yourself, your child, or your family. Take baby steps, if that is what it will take to move forward. If you want to be an engineer, then know the steps that you need to take to be an engineer.

- Look at where you are and the resources that you have and can gather to pursue your desires. Design a plan that is realistic for you. Commission and accept help from your parents, pastor, school counselors, and others who have sound wisdom and experience.

- Surround yourself with people who are positive and who have your best interest at heart — people who will help you to move outside of the box. There are many times in your life as a teen mother you are "boxed in." You may be in a financial box or an emotional box. But try to surround yourself with people who will help you to expand your horizons and move forward!

- Create a cycle of self worth and success, not despair and depression. If you move forward, your children see that, and they move forward, too.

- Never measure your success by your failures or mistakes. You are what you think you are. No matter what the situation or circumstance, "Think High and Walk Tall."

The Ella Tolliver Story

Ella Tolliver is one of the co-editors of this book. She has a Ph.D. and is currently Dean of Counseling at a college in Northern California. She is the proud mother of Vivian and her two siblings.

It is very difficult to write about this life experience. In fact, I have started and stopped several times. I was hesitant about putting my story into print because I am concerned about what people will think about me. However, I now realize that my past was necessary for me to be the person God wanted me to become. God can truly take our life experiences and work them out for good.

As I write this, I pray that this story will be a blessing in some way to young people. The ideal is to follow God's plan for your life and to retain your virginity until marriage. However, God is good and merciful and when mistakes are made, He is ready and able to forgive and set a new course. No mistake is defeating.

My story represents one of the most dramatic turning points in my life. I was fifteen, attending Franklin Jr. High School in Vallejo, California. I lived in a two-parent family, the youngest of four children. Every day, I walked past (what was then) the only car wash in Vallejo. A number of young men worked there, some full-time and others part-time after school. My girlfriends and I would stop to chat with some of the guys. One guy really stood out from the others and he finally asked for my phone number. His name was John. After several months of dating off and on, we called it "quits." We both dated other people. However, our lives kept coming back together again. He was four years older than I, but that didn't seem to matter much. We became good friends, enjoying each other's company and without realizing it, we created a bond that has lasted for over thirty-seven years.

I never related having sex with having a baby. Family planning and birth control were not topics of discussion that I ever remember having. In the 6th grade, we had classes about personal hygiene and the changes that would occur in our bodies as we went through puberty. Even though it was the early 60's, sex and sex education were not popular discussions, as they are today, at least not in my community. Because I lived in the pre-AIDS era, today's fears were not as prominent. I grew up in a middle class family, even though I didn't think so, at the time.

John, from the car wash, was still on the scene. After about 18 months of dating, we began to experiment with sex. Our experimentation led to an illness that I thought was the flu. The "flu" lasted for about three weeks. By then, my mother was extremely concerned and she felt that she should take me to the doctor. If she suspected that I was pregnant, she never said a word. After the doctor's visit, he consulted with my mother, privately, and delivered the news that I was six weeks pregnant. My mother was very polite and unmoved. She asked the doctor various questions about my care. I was in shock. It amazed me that my mother was so calm.

Once we were in the car, she began lectures number 1 through 101. My father just listened. When we got home, my mother was even calmer. In the midst of her hurt, anger, and shock, she never made me feel as if I was any less of an individual. She continued to build my self-esteem as she discussed my various options. After much personal deliberation and many family caucuses with John and without him, it was decided that we should get married. My family made it very clear that this was not my only choice. I appreciated their love and support.

I married at the age of sixteen and had my first child at seventeen. I completed my 11th grade year at Hogan Sr. High School. However, attending day school for my senior year was a little overwhelming with a six-month-old daughter. I opted to go to night school in the local Adult Education Program and completed my senior year there several months early. I stayed in contact with my high school friends and often participated in various social activities. In the meantime, I learned how to drive a stick shift and how to balance managing a home, a husband, a child, and school. My son was born when my daughter was 18 months old. I really needed to learn about birth control, and quickly! I had to learn real creativity with two babies. It was not until six years later that I had my third child, another daughter.

In 1977, when my children were 14, 13, and 8 years of age, my husband was the victim of a violent crime. He was stabbed more than 15 times, just missing his vital organs, yet it had done a great deal of damage internally and damage to his nerve cells. He was hospitalized for three weeks and went through several months of physical therapy. It was during his extensive recuperation period that I realized that if he had died, I would not have been able to support our family. My parents had suggested that I move in with them. As gracious as that offer was, I couldn't see moving my children in with my aging parents.

I had taken a few classes at Solano Community College. I made an appointment with a counselor to discuss degree programs. I did not have enough units in anything to earn a degree at that time. The counselor said that with a few more classes, I could transfer to a four-year college. I was unaware of the educational process and I had no idea what was involved. The counselor, Doris Higgins, was very patient, tolerant, and helped me to understand the educational process. I enrolled in classes where I learned to network and to develop a support system.

Two instructors, Milton Combs and Bill Thurston, helped me to excel beyond my educational expectations. They must have seen something in me that I didn't even see in myself. My husband and I decided that I should go for it. I had worked in various clerical positions, but I had to select a transferable major. Psychology appeared to be the most viable way to go. Not knowing what I would do with that as a major, it appeared to be a realistic goal.

After completing additional courses at Solano and Napa Community Colleges, I was now ready to transfer to Sonoma State. I really didn't know what transferring meant or even what a B.A. degree was. I just knew that it was higher education and that it would make me marketable, placing me in a better position to take care of my children. I completed my B.A. degree in two years, graduating with honors.

At the same time, I maintained a home, my children, my husband, and part-time employment. Had it not been for my husband's tragic ordeal, I would never have thought about higher education. My parents lived long enough to share my educational accomplishment. My mother was just as excited as I was, when I walked off the platform with my Bachelors degree. Waiting at the end of the runway was my mom, my dad, and my best friend/husband, John.

I applied for a position as a probation officer at the encouragement of a good friend who worked in the field. The pay was good and it was close to home. After going to the interview, I realized that I really didn't want to do that type of work. When they called me to take the job, I turned it down. I had heard about a Master's degree. So I began checking into local schools where a Master's could be obtained. I enrolled at California State University at Hayward in 1982. On the same day that I enrolled, my mother died.

I took a short leave, but I began school the next quarter. I completed my Master's in Counseling and Mental Health with an emphasis in Community College Counseling in 1984, with honors. Unfortunately, neither my mom nor dad lived to see this next accomplishment. I had found my niche. After completing an internship at Solano Community College, I knew that I had found an area where I could make a difference and one that I enjoyed. I could use my gift of talking, teaching, and sharing my life experiences with others as college counselor/professor. I was thrilled. I had done some part-time teaching at the elementary, junior high, and high school levels, but nothing excited me more than working with adults on the college level. I had finally set a goal for getting a Ph.D. by the time I was 50 years old. I realized that goal in 1996, when I successfully defended my dissertation at Walden University.

What had started out as a devastating experience, turned into an opportunity. My husband and I are still married. We have beaten the odds of failed teen marriages. I consider John my God-chosen mate and I realize that he was a part of God's plan for my life.

The tools that allowed my transformation include:

- A belief in God and His ultimate plan for my life; - Unconditional love and support from my family and friends; - A support system of non-critical individuals; - Opportunities for continued education; - Learning to manage my time and resources productively; - Learning to ask for help; - Rewarding myself for small and large accomplishments; - Always having high expectations for myself; and, - Having the courage to fail – if you never fail, you will never succeed.

Developing a survival plan is essential. There is an African proverb about the gazelle that woke up every morning saying that he had to run fast enough to outrun the lion, so that he wouldn't be eaten. The lion woke up every morning knowing that he had to run fast enough to outrun the gazelle so that he wouldn't go hungry. For whatever reasons, they each had a survival plan. My advice to teens is:

- Prepare yourself spiritually, educationally, and socially to meet life's challenges.

- Develop a plan and stick to it.

- Never lose sight of your dreams.

EPILOGUE

There is a close correlation between having a baby in the teenage years and poverty. Poverty is simply the inability to earn a sustainable living. Studies have shown that there is a direct correlation between education and one's ability to earn a living – the more education, the more earning power. The women in Transformations have beaten the odds. Their stories reveal proven steps to success.

The results of this project confirm the importance of education in the fight against poverty. Education clearly plays a significant role in whether or not an individual is able to become self-sufficient. The women profiled in this book were all teenagers when they became pregnant. All of them overcame barriers and achieved success, realizing their dreams and goals.

Dropping out of school, rather than merely having a baby, appears to be the key factor that sets adolescent mothers behind their peers. Many adolescent mothers drop out of school before they become pregnant. Adolescent mothers who stay in school are almost as likely to graduate (73%) as women who do not become mothers while in high school (77%), according to the Alan Guttmacher Institute.

Many things have contributed to the success of the women profiled. One common element was that of support – support from family, friends, and community. Some of the support was financial, other support was "in-kind" (free childcare, housing, etc.). Still, other support was in the form of listening, helping to resolve problems, and providing encouragement during difficult times. When teens become pregnant, we must assist them – not abandon them. On-going support is critical to their success.

There is a distinction between the struggles and issues of the mothers who were under 18 at the time of the births of their children and those who were 18 or 19 when their children were born. A year of maturity appears to make a significant difference when it comes to parenting. The response from parents, as well as from the community, is also different regarding a young woman of 18, who has completed high school.

Two individuals, who were 18 and 19 when they gave birth, had also completed over a year of college before becoming pregnant. Both of them married the fathers of their children, although they were later divorced. Two others also married the fathers of their children and both went on to have other children. Both of these remain married to their spouses after fifteen and thirty-seven years of marriage, respectively. They are living testimonials that teenaged marriages can be successful.

One-third of the teen mothers profiled in this book have parents who are college educated. Of this number, 60% come from families where both parents hold graduate level degrees. Many people make the erroneous assumption that teen mothers come from backgrounds of poverty and deprivation. Clearly, this is not always the case. Exposure to higher education also plays an important role by providing tools and access to critical life management information. Most importantly, whether parents are college educated or not, there is a high correlation between a teen parent's success and the emphasis placed on education in their homes.

Throughout the individual stories was the continuing theme of perseverance – a deep desire and a commitment to accomplishing their goals. They were unwilling to relinquish their dreams because they had become parents too soon. Many were on welfare at various stages in their experiences, but each is currently financially stable. No one interviewed currently lives at or below the poverty level.

As a result of becoming teen parents, many of the women became overachievers. Many placed a high degree of pressure on themselves to achieve success and they did! Their professional positions include: lawyer, judge, registered nurse, college professor, social worker, counselor, X-Ray technician, accountant, and military officer. At the time of this project, one young woman is entering her third year of medical school.

All of the women interviewed appear to possess the inner determination that has propelled them toward their goals. They have been focused and determined to create better lives for themselves and their children. Their determination and inner strength has enabled them to continue to move toward their goals, even when the outcomes were not apparent.

Most of the participants delayed having a second child. This enabled them to remain focused and to master providing optimum care for the child they already had. Some participants reported being avid readers as children. Most were doing well in school before their pregnancies. Thus, the basic foundation for success had already been laid. Teen pregnancy does not necessarily lead to school failure; however school failure does increase the odds of teen pregnancy.

Documenting the journey of successful teenaged moms is long overdue. While delaying pregnancy is the ideal, it is important that teens, who are currently parents, know that their lives need not be considered ended with the birth of a child. Our stories prove that the birth of a child can indeed be a rich and rewarding beginning – a transformation of sorts – a very positive TRANSFORMATION.

Living Life

by Karen M. McCord

If I had my life to live over I'd be a woman again. I love being a woman. I'd be a daughter, a sister, a friend, a grandmother, an aunt and auntie, a mother, a wife, a lover and significant other. The roles would be the same; for I've enjoyed all of my roles at one time or another, so much of who I am could remain the same.

If I had my life to live over, I'd improve my relationships with my family, parents, siblings and children. I'd be more patient, more kind, gentler, more faithful and exhibit more self-control. I'd give away fewer things and more of me. I'd spend more time working on myself and less time trying to change others. I'd travel "within" earlier in life, exploring and getting to know me.

If I had my life to live over, I'd spend more time experiencing today and not deferring to someday; I'd go without reservation embracing the opportunity to experience life from a different angle. I'd spend more time in the snow, more time on the beach, more time in the sun and yes even more time in the rain. I'd simply have more fun enjoying the sheer beauty of life. I'd spend more time in parks absorbing nature, I'd watch more sunrises and sunsets. I'd stop more just to watch the river as it flows. I'd have more mountain top experiences.

If I had my life to live over, I'd find more reasons to be happy each day. I'd find more reasons to play and more time pray. I'd skate more, ski more, cycle more, swim more, learn more, read more, play cards more, pray more, laugh more, cry more, play basketball more, love more deeply and visit more with family and friends. I'd ride more merry go-rounds and blow more bubbles in the yard and yes, even in the house! I'd learn to swim better and earlier so when my tears created a pool I'd be able to swim more swiftly through the challenges of life.

If I had my life to live over, I'd hug more and love more. I'd cultivate more joy and more peace. Yesterday has gone and tomorrow might never be… so today I must live my life being the best me. Today I must do exactly what I would do if I had life to live over. Yes, if I had life to live over, I'd do exactly what I'm doing today, so tomorrow when I look back at today I'll not be burdened with regrets from yesterday.

If I had my life to live over, I'd remain A WOMAN committed to God, family, friends and the development of a happy, peaceful, divinely purposeful life. I'd leave the handprint of a life that made a difference.

A Look in the Mirror

by Ella Clark-Tolliver

I look in the mirror, now at 50-plus, and the reflection I see is not all me.

It's my mother, my father, my sister and my brothers, too, They all find a place on my face through and through.

Not like a puzzle that fits just fine, But, rather, a movable collage with a distinct design.

But my mother's image is the one I see, Staring back so strong, urging me on, looking at, and listening to me.

It feels just fine as I linger on, This vision, a reflection that is not just mine.

My mother, my father, my sister and brothers, too, Are images, memories, and thoughts of you.

Look in your mirror. What do you see? I hope the image will help you to be, more than just a branch of the tree!

Transformations
An anthology of personal womens' stories

```
┌─────────────────────────────────────────────────────────────┐
│            Order Form           (All orders must be pre-paid)
│  Name                           Payment: Make check or money order payable to:
│                                 Teen Mothers Project
│  Company                        P.O. Box 702
│                                 Suisun City, CA 94585
│  Address
│                                        QTY. | PRICE | Subtotal
│  City                           BOOK          $12.50
│  State/Province                            Handling   $2.00
│                                 Shipping (add .50 per book)
│  Zip/Postal Code                           TOTAL
│  Phone
│
│  ☐ I am interested in a workshop or speaker presentation   ☐ I'd like more information on the Teen Mothers' Project
└─────────────────────────────────────────────────────────────┘
```